THE BOOK LOVER'S
LONDON

THE BOOK LOVER'S GUIDE TO
LONDON

SARAH MILNE

WHITE OWL

AN IMPRINT OF PEN & SWORD BOOKS LTD.
YORKSHIRE – PHILADELPHIA

First published in Great Britain in 2021 by
White Owl
An imprint of
Pen & Sword Books Ltd
Yorkshire - Philadelphia

Copyright © Sarah Milne, 2021

ISBN 9781399001144

Printed and bound by Replika Press Pvt. Ltd.
Design: Paul Wilkinson.

Pen & Sword Books Limited incorporates the imprints
of Atlas, Archaeology, Aviation, Discovery, Family
History, Fiction, History, Maritime, Military, Military
Classics, Politics, Select, Transport, True Crime, Air
World, Frontline Publishing, Leo Cooper, Remember
When, Seaforth Publishing, The Praetorian Press,
Wharncliffe Local History, Wharncliffe Transport,
Wharncliffe True Crime and White Owl.

For a complete list of Pen & Sword titles please contact
PEN & SWORD BOOKS LIMITED
47 Church Street, Barnsley, South Yorkshire, S70 2AS,
United Kingdom
E-mail: enquiries@pen-and-sword.co.uk
Website: www.pen-and-sword.co.uk

Or
PEN AND SWORD BOOKS
1950 Lawrence Rd, Havertown, PA 19083, USA
E-mail: Uspen-and-sword@casematepublishers.com
Website: www.penandswordbooks.com

CONTENTS

FOREWORD

THE LIVES OF the writers who made their homes in and frequented London are often as compelling as the stories they told. It has been said that Dickens helped to create the London we experience as sure as its actual builders did. Everyone writing about London has an exciting story to share with us about the city through their experiences, helping us to know, understand and love London and all the varied and cosmopolitan people and communities that make it.

Throughout the centuries, London's writers have lived through the Plague, the Great Fire, been bombed out of their homes in the Blitz, had affairs, been imprisoned for affairs, enjoyed raucous parties, fallen in love with each other, fallen out with each other... their lives have been every bit as colourful as their fiction.

This book is a guide to London's writers, from Geoffrey

Chaucer in 1400 up to the present day. It explores how their lives and experiences of the city shaped their writing and how we can see London through their work. There is far more to tell than can fit into this book. London's most famous writers could fill a book this size all on their own. Not every writer, not every address they have ever lived in can be included, or it would just be a long list. I have concentrated most on biographical snapshots – stories that are the most interesting and intriguing, and on bringing fictional books and scenes to life by guiding you right into their heart. I chose to write this book in such a way that it can be carried around and used as a reference and guide whilst in London, but can also be read anywhere in the world to bring the city's literature to life.

I hope this book will bring you a greater love of London and its literature. Maybe it will fire up your imagination and inspire you to write something of your own, bringing to life the London you know.

1

CENTRAL LONDON

BLOOMSBURY

Isabella Woodhouse, in Jane Austen's *Emma* (1816) declares Bloomsbury to be a part of London, 'very superior to most others.' Set in London's fashionable West End, Bloomsbury has elegant Georgian residencies, lush garden squares, stylish shops, booksellers, publishers, and all a stones-throw from the British Museum. It is no surprise Bloomsbury has become synonymous with London's literature.

The British Museum

Since it opened its doors on Great Russell Street in 1759, the British Museum has been a great source of inspiration for London's writers, with exhibits on themes such as life, death, love and money, spanning two million years and six continents. Percy Bysshe Shelley, the Romantic Poet and husband to novelist Mary, wrote his famous sonnet, *Ozymandias* during a visit when he discovered the museum had acquired a gigantic statue of Ramesses II. Russell Hoban's fantasy classic, *The Lion of Boaz-Jachin and Jachin-Boaz* (1973) was inspired by a relief of an Assyrian royal lion hunt.

More recently, the novelist Imogen Hermes Gowar wrote *The Mermaid and Mrs Hancock* (2016), a tale set in the

The dying lion from the King's Hunt Relief from the Palace of Assurbanipal in Ninevah, Assyria, that inspired Hoban's work. Flik47/shutterstock.com

The curved bookcases of the British Museum Reading Room. GTS Production/shutterstock.com

seedy side of London in the 1780s about how the lives of a merchant and a high-class prostitute come together following the arrival of a mermaid in London. The book was born from a writing exercise based around an artefact in the museum's collection: Gowar chose a Japanese work comprising of a monkey's body sewn to a fish's tail.

The British Museum was home to the British Library until 1973, when it moved to Euston Road. In 1857 it had opened its own reading room; a vast library of books and materials linked to its gallery displays. Nestled inside the museum's famous Central Courtyard, this unique dome-covered building, with its array of literature displayed on walls of curved shelving, was a nirvana for writers.

The library was a favourite place for Karl Marx and Lenin to compose their essays. When Charles Dickens acquired a reader's ticket on his eighteenth

The Reading Room is now an exhibition space in the museum's Central Courtyard. elesi/shutterstock.com

birthday in 183, he set himself the goal of researching the entire history of England and the Complete Works of Shakespeare. Bram Stoker, James Joyce and Arthur Conan Doyle would also visit frequently to research. Sherlock Holmes visits the reading room to consult a book on voodooism in *The Adventure of Wisteria Lodge* (1917).

In Peter Ackroyd's intriguing novel, *Dan Leno and the Limehouse Golem* (1994), a murder-mystery setting real historical characters in a reimagined Victorian London, Karl Marx, George Gissing and the comedian Dan Leno are all working together in the reading room, a place referred to in the book as, the 'true spiritual centre of London'.

Bloomsbury's Writers

Percy Bysshe Shelley and his wife-to-be Mary lived at 87 Marchmont Street, then a dilapidated area of Bloomsbury, between 1815 and 1816. It was here where Mary outlined *Frankenstein* (1818) and gave birth to their son, William. In 1816, Shelley's ex-wife drowned herself in Hyde Park's Serpentine River. Percy and Mary married in an attempt to secure custody of his children.

87 Marchmont Street, where Percy Bysshe and Mary Shelley lived in Bloomsbury.

Woburn Walk today. Chrispictures/shutterstock.com

W. B. Yeats lived at 5 Woburn Walk between 1895 and 1919, where he hosted a literary group attended by the likes of T. S. Elliot and John Masefield. Yeats lost his virginity here to the novelist, Olivia Shakespear, and had to buy a bed from a nearby store especially for the occasion.

Dickens' Bloomsbury

The Dickens family moved to 147 Gower Street in Christmas 1823, when Charles was eleven. His father, John, had fallen into debt and his mother opened the house as a school to earn money. 'Mrs Micawber's Boarding Establishment for Young Ladies', in *David Copperfield* (1850) is based on memories of 'Mrs Dickens' Establishment'. Unfortunately, the Dickens' school was not successful, and John Dickens was jailed at Marshalsea, a notorious prison in Southwark.

Charles Dickens.
From Meyers Lexicon Books
/shutterstock.com

In 1851, Dickens returned to Bloomsbury with his wife Catherine and their children. Dickens once became so angry after a row he stormed out at two in the morning and walked more than thirty miles to his second home in Kent. Despite the turbulence, Dickens wrote some of his best loved novels at Tavistock House, *Bleak House* (1853), *Hard Times* (1854), *Little Dorrit* (1857) and the start of *A Tale of Two Cities* (1859). In 1852, Catherine gave birth to the couple's tenth child, Edward. Children's author, Hans Christian Andersen often stayed here with the family on holidays, and Dickens' good friend Wilkie Collins often visited, staging plays with Dickens in a back room. The cloud of Charles and Catherine's continuing marital decline eventually led to their separation in 1858 and Dickens sold the house. Tavistock House was demolished in 1901 and is now the site of the British Medical Association Headquarters.

Virginia Woolf's Bloomsbury

Virginia (then Virginia Stephen), together with her sister Vanessa and brothers Adrian and Thoby, moved from their Kensington home to 46 Gordon Square

The British Medical Association Headquarters on Tavistock Street now occupies the space that was once the Dickens family home. Phaustov/shutterstock.com

in 1904, a move prompted by their father's death. The Stephen children had already lost their mother, and their father had been the one to encourage Virginia to write professionally. The Bloomsbury Group grew out of the free-thinking, free-spirited life the siblings and their friends

Virginia Woolf. VW/shutterstock.com

were able to adopt in the Bloomsbury of the 1900s.

The Bloomsbury Group was a group of writers, intellectuals, artists and philosophers who lived, studied or worked in and around Bloomsbury in the first half of the twentieth century. The male members were Cambridge University friends and associates of Thoby Stevens. They included the art critic, Clive Bell, who married Vanessa, the novelist E. M. Forster, biographer Lytton Strachey and the essayist, Leonard Woolf, who Virginia married in 1912. The group were heavily influenced by the Cambridge Philosopher, G. E. Moore's idea that key goals in life should be to create and appreciate things of beauty and engage in the pursuit of knowledge.

The Bloomsbury Group first came together at 46 Gordon Square. Here they gathered to discuss, debate and dissect literature and art, encourage one another's projects and promote each other's work.

In 1918, with support and encouragement from the group, Strachey published his most famous and important work *Eminent Victorians*. He moved into 51 Gordon Square in 1921 and stayed until his death in 1932.

The Bloomsbury Group made a huge impact on London's literature and were also portrayed in fiction themselves. They were on the receiving end of Wyndham Lewis' savage humour in his 1930 novel *Apes of God,* a satirical depiction of London's contemporary art and literature scene. Vanessa and Virginia were the inspiration for the bohemian and intellectual Schlegel sisters in E. M. Forster's novel, *Howards End* (1910). Woolf herself depicted her Bloomsbury life and the group in her

Number 51 Gordon Square, Lytton Strachey's Bloomsbury Home. Bas Photo/shutterstock.com

first novel *The Voyage Out* (1915), which follows Rachel on a modern mythical adventure from a sheltered life in a London suburb through intellectual conversation and stimulation, to self-discovery. The novel refers to a London group that meets to talk about art. The novel is likely to have been inspired by Woolf's own journey from a cloistered household to the new life she found through the liberal, intellectual stimulation in the Bloomsbury Group.

In 1924 Virginia and Leonard Woolf returned to Bloomsbury, to 52 Tavistock Square, following a decade in Richmond, Surrey. Virginia's delight at being back in London inspired her to write *Mrs Dalloway* (1925), a book set over one day in high-society Westminster, following Mrs Dalloway as she goes about shopping, preparing and hosting a party, while reminiscing her life. Woolf also wrote her famous essay on women in literature, *A Room of One's Own* (1929), here as well as her novels, *To The Lighthouse* (1927) and *The Waves* (1931).

The Bloomsbury Group were known for their liberal views on sexuality. Woolf became friends with Vita Sackville-West, a fellow author, ten years her junior. In 1925, the couple began a romance that lasted a decade. Woolf's experiences with Sackville-West inspired *Orlando: A Biography* (1928), a book she wrote for her lover. It tells of Orlando's adventures in love across 300 years, during which the character transforms from an Elizabethan lord to a 1920s London lady.

A bust of Virginia Woolf stands in the middle of Tavistock Square. Alan Kean/shutterstock.com

The book is still influential as the first English language trans novel.

In 1939, Virginia and Leonard left London for Sussex. A year later the Tavistock house was destroyed in the Blitz. The house lay in ruins for several years, displaying the couple's scorched and damaged books, art and other possessions that had been left behind in London. The Tavistock Hotel now stands on the site.

Orwell's Bloomsbury

Throughout the end of the nineteenth century, poet W. H. Davies wandered across the UK, America and Canada, living the life of a tramp. The playwright George Bernard Shaw befriended him and helped him find his way back into society, and Davies moved to 14

Russel Street where he lived from 1916 to1922. Davies' *The Autobiography of a Super-Tramp* (1908) inspired George Orwell to experience the destitute and lawless end of London's society himself, sleeping rough with vagrants in the East End, Embankment and Trafalgar Square.

In 1923, Orwell had his first professional writing job at *The Adelphi*, the English literary journal based on Bloomsbury Street. Between 1941 and 1943 he worked for the government's Ministry of Information, in Malet Street's towering, white brick Senate House. During the Second World War, the Ministry controlled the publication of information and promoted propaganda. This provided a great opportunity for London's writers. Orwell prepared propaganda for the BBC. His wife, Eileen, worked in the Ministry of Food.

The novelist Graham Greene joined for the Ministry in 1940 and was tasked to write a short story for the US magazine, *Colliers*, to convince sceptical Americans they would do best in the war by fighting alongside their brave British allies. Greene wrote *The Lieutenant Died Last*. The story was developed into the 1942 propaganda film *Went the Day Well*, before being published in Greene's short story collection, *The Last Word and Other Stories*, in 1990, shortly before his death in 1991.

John Betjeman worked in the Ministry's film division and was almost sacked for mocking a colonel. Dylan Thomas applied for a job but, after admitting he was barely able to work out other people's poems and had no understanding of any foreign language, was given a job with Strand Films in Soho instead.

The looming Senate House, together with the propaganda, secrecy and censoring that went on inside its walls, became the inspiration for Orwell's 'Ministry of Truth' in his famous dystopian novel *1984* (1949)

Senate House also appears in John Wyndham's *The Day of the Triffids* (1951) where it is temporarily taken over as the London headquarters for the sighted survivors. For over forty years, John Wyndham lived at 'The Penn Club', a Quaker-oriented, private members club, first on Tavistock Square and then at its

Senate House. Wei Huang/shutterstock.com

current address at 21–23 Bedford Place. For many years he lived in the room next door to his wife and fellow member, Grace Wilson, a rare arrangement as men and women were usually separated on different floors. Wyndham wrote all his best-known novels at the club, including *The Day of the Triffids* and *The Midwich Cuckoos* (1957).

In 1950, Orwell died in University College Hospital on Gower Street, suffering a burst lung caused by tuberculosis. He had married his second wife, Sonia Bronwell, in the hospital a few weeks before as he believed he would recover and wanted to take her to the countryside where neighbours would not approve of their out-of-wedlock affair. The marriage needed special permission from the Archbishop of Canterbury due to an ancient law protecting a dying millionaire from a potential gold digger. The hospital has since developed and grown but the entrance used in Orwell's day remains as the entrance to the Accident and Emergency department.

The University College, next door to the hospital, on Gower Street, was where Griffin, *The Invisible Man* studied medicine in H. G. Wells' 1897 novella. Griffin's cover was first blown on Great Russell Street, when a couple of street children notice footprints magically appearing in the mud.

The young Jack Rose in Jonathon Kemp's ingenious *London Triptych* (2010) first meets the pimp Alfred Taylor at his boys-house on Fitzroy Street. Alfred

University College Hospital, where George Orwell died in 1950. Willy Barton/shutterstock.com

University College London, where 'The Invisible Man' studied medicine. Orskis/shutterstock.com

Taylor, the co-defendant in Oscar Wilde's trial for gross indecency, ran a male brothel here in the 1890s and introduced many of his young men to Wilde. *London Triptych* retells the story from the perspective of Taylor's boys who were involved with Wilde. This story is weaved around the tale of an Islington artist in 1954, and Jack in 1998, enjoying the liberation of life in modern-day London. The book takes a detailed and atmospheric journey across most of London and is rich with its history.

Fitzroy Street where Alfred Taylor ran his male brothel and often introduced Oscar Wilde to his rent boys.

Bloomsbury's Publishing World

Faber and Faber have been based in Bloomsbury since 1921. T. S. Eliot worked at their office on Russell Square between 1925 and 1965, as a literary advisor then editor. Eliot was instrumental in Faber becoming one of Britain's most prestigious poetry publishers. In the 1930s, Eliot's estranged wife was often seen parading outside the office in a sandwich board proclaiming, 'I am the wife that T. S. Eliot abandoned'. Eliot was often visited by colleagues, such as Dylan Thomas and Philip Larkin,

The original Faber and Faber building where T. S. Eliot worked as an editor. Patrick Comerford, 2011

desperate for publication tips. His relationship with George Orwell was not so accommodating. In his socially critical novel, *Keep the Aspidistra Flying* (1936), Orwell referred to Eliot as 'one of the squibs of the passing minute'. This was meant to be tongue-in-cheek but, in 1944, Eliot turned down Orwell's *Animal Farm* for publication. Faber and Faber are now based at Great Russell Street.

Just around the corner, on Bedford Square, are the Bloomsbury Press, famous for accepting J. K. Rowling's *Harry Potter and the Philosopher's Stone* (1997) after it had been rejected by twelve other publishers.

Bloomsbury paid just £2,500 for the first adventure of the boy wizard, Harry Potter, and ran just 500 original copies. Wachi Wit/shutterstock.com

SOHO

Soho is just down the road from the genteel squares of Bloomsbury. It was once a desirable district for the aristocracy, but as neighbouring areas, like Mayfair and Marylebone, became more fashionable during the nineteenth century, Soho slid into neglect and its aristocratic homes were replaced by prostitute dens, drinking houses, theatres and music halls. This brought an eclectic mix of migrants, outsiders, academics, artists and writers to the area, resulting in a unique sub-culture of ideas, languages and sexuality that feature in a myriad of poems, novels and memoirs.

Blake's Soho

William Blake was born in 1757 in a workhouse on Marshall Street, situated directly behind Broad Street (now Broadwick Street). It is believed that Blake's bleak early memories of Soho inspired *Songs of Innocence and Experience* (1789) and some of his most famous lines of all, such as the 'dark satanic mills,' in Jerusalem. The house was demolished in 1965 but the building on its former site is named 'William Blake House' and is marked by a plaque, so you can pause and imagine how Soho must have been for Blake back in the days of mills and workhouses. It wasn't just in his writing that Blake turned to Soho for inspiration. Blake developed his unique and revolutionary printing technique in a narrow, four storey house at 28 Poland Street. This enabled him to place text and image on the same page for the first time, something that enabled him to combine his work as a writer and artist and came to determine the distinctive style that still sets him apart to this day.

William Blake.
Morphart Creation, Shutterstock

Dickens' Soho

Dickens was a regular visitor to Soho during its transition from a fashionable aristocratic quarter to a centre for entertainment, drink and revelry. The House of St Barnabas, at Number One Greek Street, cornering Soho Square, is recognisable by its distinctive band of jumbled red and yellow tiles spelling 'House of Charity'. When Dickens first visited Soho the house was owned by Joseph Bazalgette, the engineer who helped end cholera by building London's sewer works, still in use today. The House of Charity moved here in 1862 and has remained a base for various charities. It is now a unique blend of a private members' club funding its charitable work as an employment

Manette Street, Soho.

The House of St Barnabas, the inspiration for the home of the Manettes in A Tale of Two Cities (1859).
Alena Veasey/shutterstock.com

agency for homeless Londoners.

Dickens chose the house as inspiration for the home of Dr Manette and his daughter, Lucie, in his novel, *A Tale of Two Cities* (1859). The tree Dr Manette and his daughter entertained beneath still stands in the Courtyard. Dickens describes Manette's home as on quiet street corner, 'not far from Soho Square'. The House of St Barnabas' gardens back onto a small street linking Greek Street to Charing Cross. Formally Rose Street, the street was renamed Manette Street.

In the early 1800s, Regent Street became the dividing line between Soho, now in social and economic decline, and stylish and affluent Mayfair. By the mid-nineteenth century, Regent Street had become a fashionable residence for the upper class. Dickens made Regent Street the home of rich, young nobleman, Lord Frederick Verisopht in *Nicholas Nickelby* (1839).

Soho's Seedier Shades

Robert Louis Stevenson was one of the earliest writers to depict Soho's seedy world of misfits, in his famous novella *The Strange Case of Dr Jekyll and Mr Hyde* (1886). The book was influenced by the scientific discourses of the Late Victorian Era and centres on the split personality of the respected Dr Jekyll and his violent alter ego, Mr Hyde. Stephenson used location as a way of depicting two characters in a single man. Dr Jekyll lived in a reputable Georgian

Regent Street.
Marton Kerek/ shutterstock.com

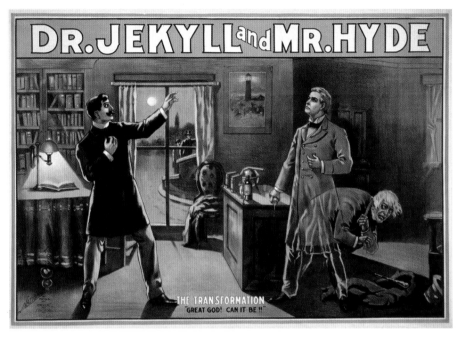

A theatrical poster showing the lawyer, Utterson, observing Dr Jekyll transform into Mr Hyde.
shutterstock.com

townhouse in Cavendish Street 'the citadel of medicine', just off Oxford Street. In contrast, the hazy, alcoholic, entertainment district of Soho was used as the sordid backdrop for Mr Hyde's debauched behaviour.

Sex and criminal activities

In *The Secret Agent* (1907), Joseph Conrad gave his central character, the Russian spy, Mr Verloc, a seedy Soho backstreet sex shop to run as a front to hide his espionage and plotting.

Colin MacInnes depicts Soho as an area of casual sex, violence and racial tension in his London trilogy of novels: *City of Spades, Absolute Beginners* and *Mr Love and Justice* (1957–1960). Soho's

Soho's seedy side has inspired come colourful scenes in London's literature. Christo Mitkov Christov/shutterstock.com

Soho's Chinatown.
vvoe/shutterstock.com

shadier scene wasn't just confined to the imaginations of its writers. Novelist Graham Greene was known to frequently slip out of his flat in St James and descend upon Soho's vice clubs and bars during the 1950s. Soho prostitutes often appear in Greene's novels.

In Timothy Mo's novel *Sour Sweet* (1982) a 1970s Chinese family try to succeed as restaurateurs in Soho's Chinatown whilst battling its ruthless world of organised crime and the sinister activities of 'The Triads'.

The essayist, Thomas De Quincy, author of *Confessions of an English Opium Eater* (1821), lodged at 61 Greek Street when he arrived in London in 1802 as a penniless teenager. De Quincy bought his first opium in 1804 from a pharmacist, then at 173 Oxford Street. His first purchase was to relieve the pain of facial neuralgia, but by 1816, opium mixed with brandy had become a daily ritual.

De Quincy wrote his famous essay at

The site of De Quincy's chemist, now occupied by Marks and Spencer. Ink Drop/shutterstock.com

his later home in Tavistock Street. The book was an immediate success and serialised in *The London Magazine,* but De Quincy blew the money on more opium.

A Bohemian Utopia

While may writers have found inspiration in Soho's sordid underworld of sex and criminal activities, the enjoyment of Soho's revelry has coloured the lives and works of many of its writers. By the mid-twentieth century Soho was fast becoming a bohemian utopia. Against the backdrop of post-war rationing and pubs closed from mid-afternoon, Soho was rising as a thriving counterculture, where intellectuals, immigrants and outsiders came together in cafés and prohibition bars to create a melting pot of ideas, languages, traditions and sexuality. Here, some of the most revered artists of the time were able to create an alternative vision of life and the world, a world that was perfect for writers.

Much of Soho's cultural and artistic life centred around The Colony Room Club, at 41 Dean Street, opened by Muriel Belcher in 1948, who secured a licence for the Colony as a private club where patrons could drink legally through the day until the scandalous hour of 11.30pm. Muriel Belcher, and her Jamaican girlfriend, Carmel Stuart, had a knack for attracting colourful people and The Colony quickly became the

Soho has remained a vibrant and varied area of London.
Christo Mitkov Christov/ shutterstock.com

41 Dean Street, where the famous Colony Room once was, is now Ducksoup, a popular restaurant.
Joas Souza/shutterstock.com

chosen drinking den and hangout for artists, poets, writers and free thinkers. These included the writers Noël Coward, E. M. Forster and Tallulah Bankhead. All of these writers included themes of debauchery and sexuality in their works, doubtlessly inspired by the Colony. The editor of Poetry London invented the term 'Sohoitis' to warn writers not to spend too much time there if they actually wanted to get any work done.

Soho's Bars and Drinking Houses

Soho's bars are the setting of many classic works, and the setting of many a story about their writers. The 1920s and 1930s saw over 150 drinking houses and clubs open in Soho, and Noël Coward is thought to have visited most! In the 1940s and 1950s, the area's cosmopolitan mix bought vibrant jazz clubs, expresso bars and drinking inns. Many of these survived Soho's sleazier period in the 1970s. In recent years, the sex shops and establishments have been replaced with gay clubs and designer bars and the area has risen again to become one of London's most fashionable quarters. A walk into many of Soho's bars can take your right into the world of its great writers and, as the area has remained popular among London's creatives, you may well find yourself rubbing shoulders with popular writers of today.

Café Royal, 68 Regent Street

The Café Royal opened on Regent Street in 1865 and soon became one of High Society London's top places to be seen, attracting writers such as Oscar Wilde,

The Café Royal.
Josepizarro/shutterstock.com

D. H. Lawrence, Graham Greene, George Bernard Shaw and Virginia Woolf. Enid Bagnold, author of *National Velvet* (1935), lost her virginity here to Frank Harris, former editor of Vanity Fair, after he told her 'Sex is the gateway to life'.

Some of the key moments in one of London literatures most famous and gripping sagas happened at the Café Royal. In 1891, Oscar Wilde, then thirty-eight, met the student and budding poet, Lord Alfred Douglas, at a tea party. Wilde was charmed by the young man and showered him with letters, presents and invites, including to stay in his home and in hotels together. The Marquess of Queensbury, Douglas' father, became concerned about his son's relationship and suspicious of Wilde's intentions. In February 1896, four days after his plans to disrupt the opening of *The Importance of Being Earnest* were foiled, Queensbury left a calling card in one of Wilde's favourite members' clubs: 'To Oscar Wilde, posing somdomite' (complete with spelling error). Wilde sued Queensbury for libel, but evidence presented during the case led to his own arrest.

Douglas introduced Wilde to his father at The Café Royal where during

'Oscar Wilde in Flamboyant Costume'. A portrait by Napoleon Sarony. The Everett Collection/shutterstock.com

a long evening of charm, and liquor, he allayed Queensbury's fears for a while. Four years later, Oscar Wilde was in the same café, arguing with his friend and biographer, Frank Harris, over his plan to sue Queensbury for libel. Harris warned him, 'They are going to prove sodomy against you' and advised his friend to escape to France. Wilde ignored him and stormed out. The argument was witnessed by George Bernard Shaw, who referred to it in the preface to his play, *The Lady of the Sonnets* (1910).

The real-life stories of London writers at the café were colourful enough but it also features in their fiction. John Buchan was a regular visitor and has Richard Hannay dining at The Café Royal in the opening of *The Thirty-Nine Steps* (1915). Sherlock Holmes was nearly murdered by men with sticks outside the café in Sir Arthur Conan Doyle's *The Illustrious Client* (1925).

Dean Street Townhouse, 69–70 Dean Street

Dean Street Townhouse is situated in the heart of Soho. The site has been standing since 1732–1735. Once homes for aristocratic families, including King Charles II's mistress Nell Gwynne, it was later refashioned as a drinking house, attracting sculptors, architects and artists. Noël Coward was among the regulars there and often gave performances, as well as drinking late into the night. It is now a lavish bar, hotel and restaurant but is worth spending money and time here to imagine what it was like in Coward's time and for all the many other writers who have been in these rooms and, no doubt, inspired by them.

The French House, 49 Dean Street

Just along the street from the Townhouse is The French House, a legendary and friendly pub where music, television and mobile phones are banned in favour of good, old-fashioned conversation. The pub was opened in 1891 as The York Minster, but was renamed after becoming a favourite meeting place for the French Resistance in the Second World War. The pub has always been popular with London's writers. Dylan Thomas famously left the manuscript for his 1954 radio play, *Under Milk Wood* under his chair in the bar, while under the influence of

The French House, Dean Street Soho.
C K Travels/shutterstock.com

ale. Thankfully, he was reunited with his classic work!

It is believed that the poet and novelist, Sylvia Plath, signed the publishing contract for her famous collection *Ariel* (1965) here.

Quo Vadis, 26–29 Dean Street

This restaurant and members' club was once a residential house and home to Karl Marx, who lived at number 28 between 1851 and 1856. Marx divided his time between research and writing at The British Museum and drinking in the bars and clubs around Soho, meeting with working societies and communist groups.

Leicester Square

Leicester Square was originally a gentrified area occupied by the aristocracy. It became more downmarket in the eighteenth century, and in the nineteenth century evolved as a centre of entertainment, when several major theatres were built. The Victorian heyday of Leicester Square's theatre land is poignantly captured in Sara Waters' *Tipping the Velvet* (1998), when Nan King basks in the exhilarating and lavish theatres as she first arrives in London with the male impersonator, Kitty. Nan's delight in the theatres drives her to try a career in London's music halls. When Kitty leaves, Nan returns to Leicester Square where she finds herself working as a rent boy.

In P. G. Wodehouse's *The Code of the Woosters* (1938) Bertie is arrested at Leicester Square after stealing a policeman's helmet.

Leicester Square's theatres have now been replaced by flagship cinemas, restaurants and fast food chains.
4kclips/shutterstock.com

COVENT GARDEN, CHARING CROSS AND TRAFALGAR SQUARE

Covent Garden was known for its flower, fruit and vegetable market until the 1970s. The market squares now host flea, art, craft and antique markets surrounded by fashionable shops, cafés, bars and restaurants.

Covent Garden Market

In Charles Dickens' *Oliver Twist* (1838) Bill Sikes talks of Covent Garden as a place where he can take his pick of boys to recruit into Fagin's gang.

David Copperfield (1849) buys flowers for Dora from the flower market and in *The Pickwick Papers* (1836) Job Trotter sleeps in one of the

Covent Garden Stall Holders enjoying a quiet moment with a book. Pegasus Pics/shutterstock.com

Flowers for sale in today's Covent Garden Market.
Christion Bertrand/shutterstock.com

Covent Garden's Apple Market is now a flea and art market.
LongJon/shutterstock.com

market's vegetable baskets. In *Great Expectations* (1860) Pip spends a more comfortable night in a Covent Garden Hotel and Arthur Clennam finds lodgings here in *Little Dorrit* (1855).

Bow Street Police Station

Bow Street, a small street by Covent Garden Square now occupied by the Royal Opera House, was home to Bow Street Police Station and Magistrates Court from 1760 till 2006. This is where the Artful Dodger is bought after being caught stealing a handkerchief from a gentleman's pocket in *Oliver Twist* (1838). In *Barnaby Rudge* (1841) Rudge is brought here for his part in the Gordon Riots, before being sent to Newgate Prison. In Arthur Conan Doyle's *The Man with the Twisted Lip* (1891) Sherlock Holmes discovers here that the beggar Hugh Boone is really Neville St Clair in disguise, the man he is under suspicion of murdering.

Oscar Wilde was brought to Bow

The Royal Opera House. Willy Barton/shutterstock.com

Bow Street Police Station. Paul Wishart/shutterstock.com

Street in 1895 following his arrest for gross indecency. Wilde was given the rare treat of a blanket for the night and had breakfast of tea, toast and eggs brought over on a tray from the nearby Tavistock Hotel. Several of London literature's famous obscenity trials were heard by Bow Street magistrates. D. H. Lawrence's *The Rainbow* was removed from publication here in 1915, and, in 1928 the court ruled Radclyffe Hall's *The Well of Loneliness* unfit for publication. The book was finally published in 1949 but Radclyffe was no longer alive to see it.

Ben Aaronovitch's popular fantasy

applause. In *Confessions of an English Opium Eater* (1821) Thomas De Quincy talks of the Opera House as being, 'by much, the most pleasant place of public resort in London for passing an evening'.

The Garrick Club Fall Out

Charles Dickens was a member of The Garrick Club, a private members' club on Garrick Street, close to Covent Garden. His contemporary, William Makepeace Thackeray, a fellow member. Dickens and Thackeray became friends and co-wrote *The Loving Ballad of Lord Bateman* in 1839. Thackeray became jealous of his friend's increasing attention and spread rumours about his infidelities

William Makepeace Thackeray.
Everett Collection/shutterstock.com

Rivers of London series begins in Covent Garden. Peter Grant, the probationary Metropolitan Police officer, is charged with guarding a murder scene. Standing around 'like a mug' he sees a shady figure slip by and begins to take a witness statement from 'a man who is already dead'. The first book, *Rivers of London* (2011), is set mostly in Covent Garden, with the rest of the series, currently at six books, set all over London.

The Royal Opera House has stood near Covent Garden's square since 1732. In 1773, Oliver Goldsmith premiered *She Stoops to Conquer* here, bringing friends from his literary club to ensure

around the club. Dickens found out and encouraged a young journalist, Edmund Yates, to write an anonymous attack on Thackeray's work. Thackeray found out from Yates that Dickens was behind the piece and began a quarrel that nearly lasted to the death. However, the pair met randomly in a street in 1863 and shook hands to finally put the matter aside. Thackeray died a few months later.

Drury Lane

In his short story 'A Gin Shop' in *Sketches by Boz* (1837), Dickens describes nearby Drury Lane as 'filthy and miserable'. Now a vivid street in the heart of London's Theatreland, it is hard to imagine the squalor Drury Lane once was. It was hit hard by the Plague, and in his 1665 *Diary of Samuel Pepys* Pepys mentions feeling sick with apprehension after seeing two or three houses there marked with the red crosses, signifying infection. Daniel Defoe said in *A Journal of the Plague Year* (1722) that London began to take the Plague seriously when two men died on Drury Lane.

In 1809, The Theatre Royal, Drury Lane, was run by the playwright and politician, Richard Brinsley Sheridan. When the theatre burned down, Sheridan was famously sitting calmly

The Theatre Royal, Drury Lane. Claudio Divizia/shutterstock.com

drinking wine and watching from Covent Garden's Great Piazza Coffee House. A fellow customer commented on his composure to which he replied, 'Can't a fellow enjoy a drink by his own fireside?'

Jane Austen loved Shakespeare and the theatre and took the opportunity to go as much as possible while visiting her brother, Henry, in London. The Theatre Royal features in *Sense and Sensibility* (1811), where Willoughby unexpectedly meets Middleton in the theatre lobby and is heartlessly told about Marianne Dashwood's illness.

THE STRAND

Villiers Street

At twelve years old, Dickens was sent to work at Warren's Blacking Factory, then on Villiers Street, connecting The Strand with the Embankment. It was a hard time for the young boy, who earned six shillings a week for ten hard hours of work a day, pasting labels onto jars of shoe polish, but he needed the money to support his impoverished family. The cruel and difficult work conditions he witnessed here, especially among the factory's children, made a deep impression that inspired much of Dickens' later fictional works, as well as his interest in reform of the labour conditions and life for the poor. Dickens draws on the wretchedness he felt during this time for David Copperfield's experiences at Murdstone and Grinby's warehouse in *David Copperfield* (1849) and for Oliver's life at the workhouse in *Oliver Twist* (1838).

In the early 1890s, Rudyard Kipling

Villiers Street today is a far cry from the wretchedness Charles Dickens knew as a child in the blacking factory.
Claudio Divizia/shutterstock.com

The Blue Plaque commemorating Rudyard Kipling's time on Villiers Street.

rented a room above a sausage shop at 43 Villiers Street. Here he wrote his first novel, *The Light that Failed* (1891), a semi-autobiographical novel reflecting his experiences of unrequited love. Kipling married and had a nervous breakdown during his two years here.

Between 1859 and 1870, Dickens had an office at 26 Wellington Street, opposite the Lyceum Theatre on The Strand. From here, he published and sold his magazine *All Year Round,* which included contributions from writers such as Elizabeth Gaskell and his friend, Wilkie Collins. Collins' 1868 detective novel, *The Moonstone,* was first serialised in the magazine, drawing crowds waiting for the next episode. Dickens lived above his shop in the late 1860s, shortly before he died in 1870.

The Savoy

Savoy Hotel and Theatre, Strand, was a favourite place for Oscar Wilde's

The Savoy Hotel. Stu 22/shutterstock.com

regular orgies and dalliances with men and young rent boys. A chamber maid testified a 'stream of page boys delivering letters were usually kissed by Wilde' in the evidence Queensbury presented to turn around Wilde's libel case against him.

Before the Savoy was built and opened by Richard D'Oly Carte in 1889, it was the site of the more modest, Fountain Court. William Blake spent his last years in two run-down rooms, before dying in poverty in 1827.

CHARING CROSS

The Sherlock Holmes, 10 Northumberland Street

This pub is dedicated to the famous detective. While enjoying a drink in the cosy bar you can step inside a reconstruction of Holmes and Watson's famous 221B Baker Street sitting room and study. The creation was first put together for the 1951 Festival of Britain

The Sherlock Holmes Pub on Northumberland Street, Charing Cross. Alana Veasey, Shutterstock

Holmes and Watson's sitting room, recreated at The Sherlock Holmes. Joseph Sohm/shutterstock.com

by the staff of Abbey House, who occupied the famous address at the time.

Adelphi

J. M. Barrie moved from Bayswater to 3 Robert Street, Adelphi, following his divorce in 1909. Here a group of authors living in the area took shelter with him during the First World War when German Zeppelins bombed the area.

Barrie's close friend, George Bernard Shaw, lived around the corner at Adelphi Terrace, 13–15 John Adam Street, with his wife, Charlotte Payne-Townshend, between 1898 and 1906. Here, he wrote his plays, *Man and Superman* and *Major Barbara* in 1905, and *The Doctor's*

Dilemma the following year. Richard D'Oly Carte, the owner of the nearby Savoy Hotel and Theatre, where many of Shaw's plays were staged, lived in the Terrace from 1881 to 1901. The architect, Sir Arthur Blomfield, had his office here between 1864 and 1868. The author Thomas Hardy stayed here while he studied architecture with Blomfield during 1864 and 1867. The original terrace has been developed into luxury apartments, but a plaque marks the spot where so many famous people and important writers once lived.

Trafalgar Square

Trafalgar Square has long been the scene of political activity and protests. On November 13, 1887, William Morris and George Bernard Shaw were among the 200,000 who assembled here to protest against unemployment and coercion in Ireland on 'Bloody Sunday'.

Harold Pinter gave an impassioned address here against the British invasion of Iraq in 2003.

In 2020, the square became a focus for fervent protests against racism, white privilege and unequal opportunities during the global 'Black Lives Matter' (BLM) movement that followed George

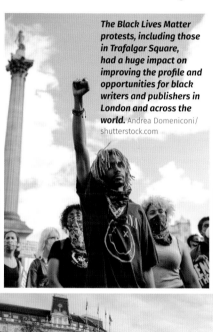

The Black Lives Matter protests, including those in Trafalgar Square, had a huge impact on improving the profile and opportunities for black writers and publishers in London and across the world. Andrea Domeniconi/ shutterstock.com

Floyd's suffocation under the knee of a US police officer. London novelist and political activist, Bernadine Evaristo, was heavily involved in the movement. In 2019, Evaristo became the first black woman to be awarded the Booker Prize, for her novel, *Girl, Woman, Other*. Following the BLM protests, she became the first black woman to top the UK fiction chart with the same book. London-born author, Zadie Smith published a collection of essays reflecting on the movement, comparing racism to the year's Covid-19 pandemic in *Imitations* (2020).

Trafalgar Square was reimagined by George Orwell as Victory Square, with Nelson's Column replaced by an imposing statue of 'Big Brother' in *1984* (1949). In Julian Barnes' *Metroland* (1980), Chris and Toni spend time at Trafalgar Square ogling women through binoculars.

Trafalgar Square.

HOLBORN AND CLERKENWELL

Backing onto the east of Bloomsbury lies Holborn, an area that includes the south-eastern end of Camden and stretches just into the City of London. Clerkenwell, east of Holborn, is a small area between the City of London and Islington. It was once a slum but has undergone waves of revival and gentrification.

Dickens' Holborn and Clerkenwell

Charles Dickens moved to 48 Doughty Street in 1837 as a twenty-five-year-old, just on the brink of making his name as a novelist. Though he only lived here two years it was a creative and productive time for the young writer. Here, Dickens completed *The Pickwick Papers* (1837), wrote *Oliver Twist* (1838), most of *Nicholas Nickleby* (1839) and began *Barnaby Rudge* (1841).

Doughty Street was a house that saw family celebrations and tragedy. The newlywed Dickens and his wife, Catherine, moved into their new home with their two-month, first born son, Charley. Catherine gave birth to their daughters Mary and Katey during their years here. The couple also shared the four-storey Georgian townhouse with Dickens' younger brother, Frederick, and Catherine's young sister, Mary, whom Dickens came to adore. Shortly after moving into their new home, the seventeen-year-old fell sick and died of heart failure in Dickens' arms. The distraught writer created Rose Maylie in *Oliver Twist* (1838) to symbolise the perfection, purity and innocence he saw

48 Doughty Street, home to Charles Dickens and his family from 1837–1839. Tuilien/shutterstock.com

in Mary. In *The Old Curiosity Shop* (1841), Little Nell's death is modelled on Mary's passing.

The Charles Dickens Museum. Alan Keon, Shutterstock

The Charles Dickens Museum allows you to walk through the family's home and see their furniture and personal possessions. Julien_j/shutterstock.com

Forty-eight Doughty Street is now home to the fascinating Dickens Museum. Here, you can experience what life was like for Dickens as he was writing his books through a tour of this family home, their rooms and personal possessions and through exhibits including original manuscripts, signed letters and notes and first editions.

Mount Pleasant Mail Centre – Coldbath Fields Prison

A short walk from Doughty Street is Mount Pleasant, home of the Smallweed family in *Bleak House* (1852), a house 'bricked in on all sides, like a tomb'. Mount Pleasant remains a densely populated street amidst the commercial and business hustle and bustle of modern Holborn and Clerkenwell. Mount Pleasant Mail Centre opened in 1900 and is one of the largest sorting offices in the world. This used to be the site of the Middlesex House of Correction, or Coldbath Fields Prison. From 1794 to 1877 this was home to 1,800 prisoners who were punished through hard labour on its merciless treadmills. Dickens held a long fascination with prisons and the lives of inmates. He became friends with Coldbath Fields' Governor, George Chesterton, who allowed him to tour the jail and see the wheels in operation, an experience Dickens describes in 'The Last Cab-Driver' in *Sketches by Boz* (1836). These visits no doubt gave Dickens invaluable inspiration that would come to life on the pages of his novels. With its terrifying gallows, Newgate Prison, in the nearby City of London, was the prison Dickens used the most when his characters faced incarceration.

Hatton Garden – Mr Fang's Court

In the second half of the nineteenth century, Hatton Garden was incorporated into Clerkenwell's exclusive and exciting Jewellery and Diamond Quarter. Hatton Garden now hosts some of the world's most expensive jewellery

Hatton Garden Jewellery Centre. CK Travels/hutterstock.com

collections and shops. From the late 1660s to the present day, the street has been the scene of many real-life heists and burglaries. With such a gripping backdrop of luxury and organised crime, Hatton Garden is the perfect inspiration and setting for London's fiction writers.

At 54 Hatton Garden was the 'very notorious' police magistrates office where Oliver Twist is sent to be tried by the ferociously cruel Mr Fang after being wrongly accused of pickpocketing Mr Brownlow. The building is now a jewellery shop, but it is easy to imagine the front parlour office, with Mr Fang sat at a desk at the far end and the terrified Oliver cowering in a wooden cage on one side.

Dickens purposely based Mr Fang on Hatton Garden magistrate, Allan Stuart Laing. Dickens was among those who protested against Laing's brutality, leading to his dismissal from the bench in 1838. Dickens' describes the police and courts in *Oliver Twist* (1838) quite intentionally as hectic and unorganised to highlight some of the problems the community were facing from the Metropolitan Police system at the time.

Hatton Garden also features in *Martin Chuzzlewit* (1844), where Mrs Gamp and Betsey Prig tend to Mr Lewisham at The Black Bull Inn. The inn has since been demolished.

The aristocratic side of Hatton Garden's diamond trade is depicted in Evelyn Waugh's novel *Brideshead Revisited* (1945) when Rex Mottram takes Julia Marchmain here to buy her engagement ring. Its criminal world is portrayed in Ian Fleming's *Diamonds are Forever* (1956), when Bond visits Rufus B. Saye, really Jack Spang, one of the controllers of the 'Spangled Mob' crime syndicate, in his Hatton Garden 'House of Diamonds'.

The Dickensian Slums of Saffron Hill

Near Hatton Garden is Saffron Hill. In Dickens' day, this was a squalid neighbourhood, home to paupers and thieves. In *Oliver Twist* (1838), the Artful

The One Tun, inspiration for The Three Cripples where Bill Sikes drinks in Oliver Twist (1838).

Dodger leads Oliver along Saffron Hill, to Fagin's den on Field Lane. Oliver experiences the street as 'wretched' place, 'narrow and muddy' and 'impregnated with filthy odours'.

Saffron Hill features heavily in the novel as the home of 'The Three Cripples', Bill Sikes' local pub. The Three Cripples was inspired by 'The One Tun' 125 Saffron Hill, where you can still enjoy ales and traditional pub food, stay a night and imagine yourself in the world of Sikes, Fagin and their associates. The Three Cripples was the name of a lodging home next door to The One Tun when Dickens was writing his novel.

In 1843, Dickens visited a Ragged School on Saffron Hill and was sickened by the felony, desperation and horrific conditions the children lived in. Dickens vowed then to help 'the poor man's child'. This experience was one of the inspirations for *A Christmas Carol* (1843), a novella that highlighted the plight of poor families and made an example of Scrooge, making him face up to his merciless ways and help the Cratchits.

Clerkenwell Green

In Dickens' day, Clerkenwell Green was an open grassy area and a popular setting for demonstrations. In November 1887, George Bernard Shaw and William Morris were among the hundreds of

Clerkenwell Green is now a built-up London Square. CK Travels/shutterstock.com

people who set off here to march on Bloody Sunday.

In *Oliver Twist* (1838) Mr Brownlow falls victim to Fagin's gang of pickpockets outside a shop on Clerkenwell Green. Oliver, shocked at what he has witnessed, is the only one left when Brownlow realises what had happened. The innocent boy is then chased through the neighbouring streets, captured and taken to Mr Fang in Hatton Garden.

The Marx Memorial Library opened at 37a Clerkenwell Gardens in 1933, on the fiftieth anniversary of Karl Marx's death. Between 1893 and 1922, the site

The Marx Memorial Library holds more than 40,000 books and papers on Marxism, Socialism and working-class history. Chris Dorney/shutterstock.com

was home to William Morris and his Twentieth Century Press, one of Britain's first socialist print works. The exiled Lenin worked here between 1902 and 1903, during which time he published his political newspaper, *Iskra*. In the 1960s, the building was saved from demolition after a campaign whose leaders included renowned poet, John Betjeman.

The Inns of Court

London's Inns of Court provide barristers with professional supervision, libraries, dining facilities and accommodation.

Gray's Inn. Spiroview Inc/shutterstock.com

Dickens worked at the inns for a time as a legal clerk and includes them in many of his novels. In *Great Expectations* (1860), Pip stays with Mr Pocket at Barnard's Inn, now Gresham College, and is bitterly disappointed to find a dingy collection of buildings rather than a cheery inn owned by a Mr Barnard!

Gray's Inn, on South Square, High Holborn, dates back as far as 1370. Elizabeth 1 was a patron and hosted parties and events here. It is thought that Shakespeare's *The Comedy of Errors* was first performed here during one of the Queen's festivals. Charles Dickens worked here as a young clerk for Ellis and Blackmore Solicitors in 1827. The building at 1 South Square, opposite Gray's Inn Hall, is still much as it would have been when Dickens was working there.

On his first day working at Gray's Inn, Dickens took his lunch break in nearby Chancery Lane. He was wearing a new cap which was mocked by a passer-by. In his anger, Dickens lashed out and received a black eye. He later used Chancery Lane as one of the main settings for *Bleak House* (1953).

The novel opens at Lincoln Inn, where Dickens compares the legal system to London's fog. At the 'very heart' of this

Chancery Lane. Bharis/shutterstock.com

dense fog, drifting all over the City, in Lincoln Inn Hall, 'sits The Lord High Chancellor in his High Court of Chancery.'

Dickens' metaphoric use of fog in many of his novels is the cause of one of the amusing episodes in Xiaolu Guo's ingenious novel *A Concise Chinese–English Dictionary for Lovers* (2007). The book follows Zhuang or 'Z' as she arrives in London, struggling simultaneously to adapt in her new city and to her new language. Having read Dickens in school, Z arrives in London and immediately looks around the sky for 'fogs'. After two days and still no fog, Z asks a policeman, 'Excuse me, where I seeing the fogs?' Z's language school is in Holborn.

Close to Gray's Inn is Furnival's Inn,

a former Inn of Court, where Charles Dickens lodged between 1834 and 1837. Following their marriage in 1836, Catherine joined him, and their firstborn,

The Great Hall, Lincoln Inn. Kievi Victor/shuttershock.com

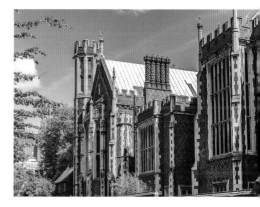

Charley, was born here in 1837. Whilst here, Dickens began writing his first novel, *The Pickwick Papers* (1836). Like many of his novels the story was originally serialised. The illustrator, Robert Seymour, often came to Furnival's Inn to discuss illustrations. During a tense meeting about the third installment, Dickens insisted that the artist changed his drawings. Seymour was upset his ideas had been rejected and was found dead in his Islington summer house two days later.

The dramatist and creator of *Peter Pan*, J. M. Barrie, lived in Furnival's Inn chambers from 1888 until just before

The bust and plaque at Holborn Bars, where Dickens once lived at Furnival's Inn.

it was demolished, after failing to pay dues, in 1889.

The site is now occupied by the red-bricked Holborn Bars, 138–142 Holborn. At the side of the building on Waterhouse Square, hiding under a terracotta canopy, is a bust of Dickens and a plaque, installed in 1907, to commemorate his time living here.

The Old Curiosity Shop

At 13–14 Portsmouth Street, not far from Lincoln Inn and tucked away among the buildings of The London School of Economics, is one of the oldest shops in London. 'The Old Curiosity Shop' dates back from the sixteenth century and survived the Great Fire of London and the Blitz. The shop is believed to have been the inspiration for Dickens' famous 1841 novel, although this is not proven, and the shop was renamed after it was published. The shop opened originally as a dairy. In the 1970s it was a bookshop, specialising in Charles Dickens books. It is currently a high-end shoe shop.

The Hospital for Children

Chares Dickens and J. M. Barrie share a generous association with Great Ormond Street Hospital for Children,. In 1858, Dickens raised money for the hospital and gave a public reading of *A Christmas Carol* here. In *Our Mutual Friend* (1865) Little Johnny dies at the hospital, 'with a kiss for the Boofer lady'.

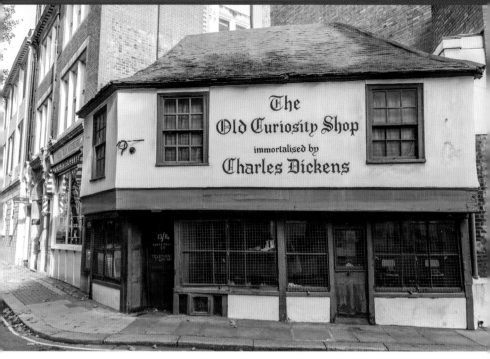

The Old Curiosity Shop was renamed after the famous novel. Alexandre Rotenberg/shutterstock.com

After graduating from Edinburgh University, Barrie moved to London to seek his fortune and landed up in lodgings on Grenville Street, just behind the hospital. The house became the inspiration for the Darlings' family home in his play *Peter Pan* (1904) and subsequent novel (1911). Barrie was a great supporter of the Children's Hospital and, in 1929, generously gifted it the copyright of *Peter Pan*. In 1988, the House of Lords recognised both Barrie's generosity and the exceptional work of his benefactors by passing a special clause in the UK's Design and Copyright

Great Ormond Street Hospital. Wael Alreweie/shutterstock.com

act, awarding the hospital indefinite rights to royalties. So, the boy who never grew up will forever live on with the children supported by one of the world's most famous Children's Hospitals.

Holborn's Poets

In the late eighteenth century, the established writer and poet, Charles Lamb, lived with his sister and co-author, Mary, in a house on Little Queen Street, now Kingsway, near Trinity Church. While there, Mary, who had a history of mental illness, stabbed her mother to death with a kitchen knife. Charles paid for Mary to be committed to a private asylum to spare her from a life in prison. The pair were best known for their children's book *Tales from Shakespeare*. Though the book was published in 1807, Mary's name did not appear on the title page until its seventh edition, in 1838.

Charles Lamb.
Morphart Creation/
shutterstock.com

In March 1956, poets Ted Hughes and Sylvia Plath spent their first night together in a flat on 18 Rugby Street, belonging to one of Hughes' Cambridge friends. The couple married later the same year at St George the Martyr in

St George the Martyr, where the poets Ted Hughes and Sylvia Plath were married in 1957. Fritz16/shutterstock.com

nearby Queen Square. Hughes recalls their first sexual encounter in *18 Rugby Street*. The poem was published just before his death in *Birthday Letters* (1998).

Clerkenwell in Modern Novels

The novelist Arnold Bennett lived most of his adult life in London. Born in the midst of Stoke-on-Trent's Potteries, his novels centred around the working-class and poverty. He was despised by his contemporaries in the Bloomsbury Group and mocked by Virginia Woolf for his matter-of-fact approach to storytelling. *Riceyman Steps* (1923) follows the final year in the life of Henry Earlforward, a miserly Clerkenwell second-hand bookseller, whose shop stands at the bottom of the steps.

Peter Ackroyd set two of his most successful novels to date in Clerkenwell. In *The House of Doctor Dee* (1993) Matthew Palmer inherits a house at 14 Farrington Lane. Palmer discovers the house was occupied by the alchemist and mystic, John Dee, during the sixteenth century and the novel weaves their stories of Clerkenwell as Palmer finds out more about the mysterious previous owner of his new home. *The Clerkenwell Tales* (2003) retells Chaucer's *The Canterbury Tales* (1400) in Ackroyd's signature style, merging fictional historical characters and past and present times.

The real Riceyman Steps can be found near Kings Cross leading up from Gwynne Place to Granville Square (Riceyman Square in the book).

THE CITY

The City of London, also known as The Square Mile, is the area of London that originally lay within the city walls of Londonium in Roman times. The City has a long and varied literary history involving many of London's most well-known and well-loved writers.

Dicken's City of London
Old Bailey and Newgate

The Central Court of England and Wales is also known as the 'Old Bailey' after the street it stands on. Dickens set many of his most memorable trial scenes here, including Fagin's in *Oliver Twist* (1838) Charles Darnay's in *A Tale of Two Cities* (1859) and that of Magwitch in *Great Expectations* (1860). The 'Bailey' also features in many thriller, mystery and

The Central Criminal Court, Old Bailey.
Bell Photography, Shutterstock

crime novels, including Julian Symons' *The Blackheath Poisoning* (1853) and many of John Mortimer's episodes of *Rumpole of the Bailey* (1978–2009).

In 1895, the Old Bailey hosted London literature's most famous trials, when Oscar Wilde was bought to trial for sodomy and indecent acts with men. Alfred Taylor, who introduced Wilde to his young boys, was also arrested. On 25 May, following a four-week trial at the Old Bailey, Wilde and Taylor were found guilty of 'unlawfully committing acts of gross indecency with certain male persons' and sentenced to two years hard labour in prison. Jonathan Kemp's *London Triptych* (2010) takes us into the court to witness the trial, when one of Taylor's rent boys, Jack Rose, is called to testify.

In 1960, The Old Bailey hosted the trial against Penguin Books for the publication of D. H. Lawrence's *Lady Chatterley's Lover*, on the grounds of obscenity. Penguin called writers including E. M. Forster and T. S. Eliot to defend the book. The Chief Prosecutor was ridiculed during the trial and Penguin were found not guilty. The trial was hugely influential and is often

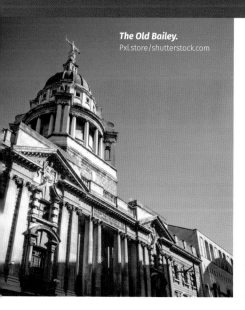

The Old Bailey.
Pxl.store/shutterstock.com

held to be the beginning of a more 'Permissive Society' in Britain.

Newgate Prison stood on the corner of Old Bailey and Newgate Street between 1188 and 1902. The site is now

The corner of Old Bailey and Newgate, once the site of Newgate Prison. Karl Weller/shutterstock.com

part of the extended Central Court. Newgate took over London's gallows from Tyburn Tree, Marble Arch in 1783 and, until 1868, executions took place in public, outside the prison on Newgate Street. Dickens campaigned strongly for the executions to be taken inside, out of public view. Dickens gives us a detailed insight into life in the prison in *Visit to Newgate* in *Sketches by Boz* (1837). In *Oliver Twist* (1938), he describes Fagin's last hours alive in Newgate, including the St Sepulchre's Church bell that would toll at eight o'clock in the morning to signal executions would be taking place that day. The church still stands on Holborn Viaduct, opposite the Old Bailey. In *Barnaby Rudge* (1841) Rudge is taken to Newgate for taking part in the Gordon Riots. Kit Nubbles is wrongly imprisoned at Newgate in *The Old Curiosity Shop* (1840).

Among London writers who have spent time in Newgate are Ben Johnson, Daniel Defoe, Chistopher Marlowe and Sir Thomas Malory. Malory wrote *Morte D'Arthur* (1585) here while serving a murder sentence. He is believed to have died in the prison, although there is some confusion around his identity. The playwright, Ben Johnson was imprisoned here for murder following a duel in North London's Hoxton. Daniel Defoe spent three days in a pillory in Newgate after being caught up in the political fall-out between the Catholic Church and James II in 1689.

Opposite Newgate, on Cock Lane,

once stood a public house, The Fortunes of War. In an upper room here corpses of executed prisoners, along with bodies stolen by grave robbers, or 'Resurrection Men' like Jerry Cruncher in *A Tale of Two Cities* (1859), were handed over to surgeons from St Bartholomew's hospital for dissection. The pub has been demolished but is its site is marked with a memorial. Dickens mentions St Bartholomew's in *The Pickwick Papers* (1836), and in *Martin Chuzzlewit* (1843) the hospital is where Sarah Gamp's nursing colleague, Betsy Prig, is based.

Scrooge and Cratchit's Cornhill Street

In *A Christmas Carol* (1843) the spirited Bob Cratchit plays with children on an ice slide on Cornhill Street 'in honour of it being Christmas Eve'. It is likely that the 'gruff old bell' that so annoys his miserable boss, Scrooge, is that of St Michael's Church, and that Newman's Court, opposite the church, is the site of the miser's counting house.

St Michael's Church is one of two churches on Cornhill Street built by Christopher Wren following the Great Fire in 1666. The other, St Peter's, is where Dickens imagined Lizzie Hexam's horrifying meeting with Bradley Headstone in *Our Mutual Friend* (1864).

On Change Alley, just off Cornhill, was Garraway's Coffee House, a popular café between 1660 and 1874. Dickens mentions this in many of his works, most famously in *The Pickwick Papers* (1836)

Cornhill today. Chrispictures/shutterstock.com

as the place where Pickwick writes his 'chops and tomato sauce' letter to Mrs Bardell.

The City's Journalism and Banking Quarters

Close to the Inns of Court and the traditional heartland of newspaper publishing, many London writers have found work in Fleet Street as journalists, lawyers and bankers.

Samuel Johnson lived at 1 Inner

Fleet Street. Georgios Antonatos/shutterstock.com

Temple Lane, off Fleet Street, in 1746 where he worked to create the first Dictionary of the English Language published in two volumes in April 1755.

T. S. Eliot worked for Lloyds Bank at nearby Cornhill Street. Virginia Woolf, who had just published Eliot's *The Waste Land* (1922) under her new Hogarth Press, encouraged him to give up banking and write full time. The Bloomsbury Group even raised a fund to

EDGAR WALLACE
REPORTER
BORN LONDON 1875
DIED HOLLYWOOD 1932
FOUNDER MEMBER OF THE
COMPANY OF NEWSPAPER MAKERS

HE KNEW WEALTH & POVERTY, YET HAD
WALKED WITH KINGS & KEPT HIS BEARING.
OF HIS TALENTS HE GAVE LAVISHLY
TO AUTHORSHIP – BUT TO FLEET STREET
HE GAVE HIS HEART.

A plaque on the corner of Fleet Street and Ludgate Circus marks the spot where the playwright Edgar Wallace sold newspapers as a twelve-year-old.
Chrisdorney/ shutterstock.com

help him to do so, but Eliot turned the offer down as he enjoyed his banking job.

P. G. Woodhouse managed the Hong Kong and Shanghai Bank on Gracechurch Street from 1900 to 1902. He was forced to resign for stealing paper to write a short story.

Fleet Street has been the setting for many stories and novels, notably Evelyn Waugh's satire *Scoop* (1936) about the unenthusiastic journalist, William Boot.

Ye Olde Cheshire Cheese, 145 Fleet Street

Ye Olde Cheshire Cheese has been a favourite for writers for hundreds of

Ye Olde Cheshire Cheese. DRG Photography/shutterstock.com

years and remains one of the pubs of choice for the city's writers and journalists to this day. Built in 1538, it burned down in the Great Fire of 1666, but was rebuilt soon after. Writers such as Samuel Johnson, Charles Dickens, Alfred Lord Tennyson, Sir Arthur Conan Doyle and P. G. Woodhouse were regulars here. The pub was once home to 'The Rhymers Club', set up by W. B. Yeats in 1890. Charles Dickens mentions Ye Olde Cheshire Cheese in *A Tale of Two Cities* (1859) and it is also mentioned in several short stories by Agatha Christie and Robert Louis Stephenson as well as in Anthony Trollope's *Ralph the Heir* (1871).

El Vino, 47 Fleet Street

Now a wine and tapas bar, El Vino was immortalised in John Mortimer's *Rumpole of the Bailey* series. It was a favourite of G. K. Chesterton who enjoyed many sessions of 'hard drinking and hard thinking' here.

The Barbican

Until the nineteenth century, Grub Street was a low-rent neighbourhood, popular with hack writers who lived among its bars and brothels. This life was immortalised in George Gissing's novel *New Grub Street* (1891), telling the tale of a writer finding his way in London at that time.

Just north of Holborn, was a now demolished house on Bunhill Road, where John Milton finished his epic poem, *Paradise Lost* (1667) and wrote the

Bohemian Grub Street has now been replaced by Milton Street's glass faced office blocks and the Barbican Estate, Barbican Centre and London Museum. Jordi Prats/shutterstock.com

follow up, *Paradise Regained* (1671). John Dryden visited in February 1674, seeking permission to rewrite *Paradise Lost* as a rhyming opera. Milton consented and suffered the embarrassment of Dryden's version outselling his own classic work. Milton died in his home here later in 1674.

John Milton.
Morphart Creation/
shutterstock.com

Bunhill Fields

Not far from Milton's home, nesting in the shadows of the City's towering offices, is the disused graveyard, Bunhill Fields. Daniel Defoe described in *A Journal of the Plague Year* (1722) how the fields opened up as a mass burial site for the victims of the 1600 plague, some of whom were thrown into the huge pits before they were actually dead. Defoe himself was buried here in 1731, in a grave marked 'Mr Dublow', following an inscription error by the cemetery clerk. John Bunyan was buried here in 1688. He was a rare visitor to London but died here from a fever caught in heavy rain. William Blake was buried in 1827 in a grave that is often adorned with flowers, a mark of his popularity and influence to this day.

Through the railings at Bunhill Fields.
Phaustou/shutterstock.com

William Blake's Grave, Bunhill Fields.
Alan Kean, Shutterstock

All three graves can be found in the central, paved area of the fields. J. B. Priestley pays tribute to the three writers in his London novel *Angel Pavement* (1930). Mr Smeeth peers through the iron railings at the 'old graves' and a passer-by tells him Defoe, Bunyan and Blake, 'lie in the sooty earth while their dreams and ecstasies still light up the world.'

WESTMINSTER

In 1802, William Wordsworth wrote his famous, 'Upon Westminster Bridge' after crossing it with his sister, Dorothy. Though the view is still, no doubt, 'touching in majesty', where the poet saw 'ships, towers, domes, theatres and temples' now stand the Houses of Parliament, Big Ben, St Thomas' Hospital and New Scotland Yard.

Parliamentary Politics and Politicians

Home to the Houses of Parliament and Downing Street, Westminster has had many books written about it, mostly recounting or reimagining the antics behind the closed doors of the British Government. Numerous writers have had the advantage of witnessing the British political system first-hand, either sitting as a Member of Parliament (MP) or working for one of Westminster's government offices. Geoffrey Chaucer

Parliament has provided valuable inspiration for London's writers, especially for satire. Rohan Bhatt/shuterstock.com

Today's view from Westminster Bridge.
Mistervlad/shutterstock.com

sat in parliament in 1386. Samuel Pepys had two terms as an MP in the 1670s and 1680s.

Philip Hensher's *Kitchen Venom* (1996) retells Parliament, during the final days of Margaret Thatcher's era, as a place of betrayal and passion where rent boys and murder are rife. Unsurprisingly the book lost Hensher his job as a House of Commons Clerk. Another insider, Michael Dobbs, put pen to paper to doodle about his experiences in Parliament, simply as a 'holiday distraction' and ended up creating one of modern literature's most famous series. Dobbs started working for the Conservative Party in 1977 and served as Margaret Thatcher's Chief of Staff from 1986 to 1987. When the two fell out during a cabinet meeting, exactly one week before the 1987 General Election, Dobbs left his job and went on holiday with his wife, where he began scribbling thoughts and ideas. His musings led to the political thriller *House of Cards* (1989), the first book in the Francis Urquhart trilogy. Dobbs, who had never set out to become a writer, has written twenty thrillers to date, including *Winston's War* (2002), the first in a four-book series about the famous wartime Prime Minister.

The prime minister's famous address, 10 Downing Street, has had links with London's literature since the very beginning. The house was presented by George II to Sir Robert Walpole, the first modern-style prime minister, in 1732. Walpole's youngest son was the writer and historian, Horace Walpole, who penned *The*

Number 10 Downing Street has a long link with London's literature. Zjstmath/shutterstock.com

Castle of Otranto (1764), the first English language Gothic novel and one of the earliest literary horror stories. The writer and politician Benjamin Disraeli served as prime minister twice in the early 1800s.

Fictional occupants of Number 10 include Plantagenent Palliser's *The Prime Minister* (1876). Downing Street is also mentioned in Evelyn Waugh's *Vile Bodies* (1930) where he imagines 'midnight orgies at no. 10'.

Westminster is home to many government offices and teams of civil servants. John Buchan was Director of Information during the First World War and recruited fellow novelists, Anthony Hope, Arnold Bennet and Somerset Maugham. Ian Fleming worked in The Admiralty, Whitehall, as personal assistant to the Director of Naval Intelligence.

Many writers worked at the Foreign Office during the Second World War. Novelist Antonia White, author of *Frost in May* (1933), an autobiographical novel

Admiralty House, Whitehall, where Ian Fleming gained invaluable experiences about the secret services to use in his James Bond books. Tupungato/shutterstock.com

The Foreign Office, where many writers worked in the Second World War. NM Bear/shutterstock.com

about growing up in a London convent school, worked alongside Graham Greene in the Political Intelligence Department. Anti-Stalinist George Orwell collaborated with the Foreign Office at the beginning of the Cold War in the late 1940s. Orwell helped draw up a blacklist of writers thought to be communists and sympathisers.

Opposite Parliament, Westminster Abbey is one of Britain's most important and well-known religious buildings. In 1399, Geoffrey Chaucer took a job as 'Master of the Kings Works', with responsibility for the abbey's upkeep and maintenance, and moved into a

Westminster Abbey. Claudio Divizia/shuttlestock.com

include those to William Wordsworth, W. H. Auden, D. H. Lawrence and Noël Coward. The last to writer to be commemorated in Poets' Corner was Ted Hughes in 2011. A floor stone dedicated to Philip Larkin was added in 2016, on the thirty-first anniversary of his death.

Poets' Corner has been criticised for overlooking women and writers of colour. Only eight women are commemorated: the Brontë sisters, Fanny Burney, George Eliot, Elizabeth Gaskell and Jane Austen. Elizabeth Barrett-Browning is also one of the eight, although there is some controversy in that she is remembered with an inscription on Robert Browning's grave: 'His wife Elizabeth Barrett-Browning is buried in Florence.' This perhaps overshadows her place as a writer in her own right with her status as his wife.

Buckingham Palace

One of London's most famous and loved characters, Paddington Bear, visits Buckingham Palace to watch the Changing of the Guard in Michael Bond's, *Paddington at the Palace* (1986). The excited bear is mistaken for a guardsman's busby and then invited through the gates to get a better view, where he is sure he gets a glimpse of the Queen through the window. In Sue Townsend's *The Queen and I* (1992) a revolutionary government forces the Queen to abdicate and relocate her family to a 'two up, two down' mid terrace house in the north of England.

house in the Abbey's gardens, where the Henry VII chapel now stands. He died here, just after completing *The Canterbury Tales* (1400) and, as a resident, became the first writer to be buried at the abbey.

Since then, many more have been buried, interned or commemorated around Chaucer's grave in the area now known as Poets' Corner. Here you can find graves and memorials for many famous writers. William Shakespeare's *Henry VI Part One* (1590) opens in the Abbey with the funeral of Henry V. Charles Dickens and Thomas Hardy are among those buried here. Memorials

Poets' Corner,
Westminster Abbey.
Dean and Chapter of
Westminster

DYLAN THOMAS
4 OCTOBER 19__
Time held me green and dying
Though I sang in my chains like the sea
Buried at Laugharne

GEORGE
ELIOT
Mary Ann
Evans
1819–1880
Buried at Highgate
Quís non reliquit.

WYSTAN
HUGH
AUDEN
1907–1973
In the prison of his days
Teach the free man
how to praise
Buried at
Kirchstetten
Lower Austria

LEWIS
CARROLL

HENRY
JAMES
O·M
Novelist
New York 1843
London 1916

A·M·D·G
ESSE QVAM VIDERI
GERARD
MANLEY
HOPKINS
S·J
1844·1889
Priest & poet
Immortal diamond
Buried at Glasnevin Dublin

Buried at
Kirchstetten
Lower Austria
JOHN MASEFIELD
O.M.
1878 ~ 1967
POET LAUREATE

THOMAS
STEARNS
ELIOT
O·M·
ORN 26 SEPTEMBER 1888
IED 4 JANUARY 1965
'the communication
tongued with fire beyond

ALFRED
LORD TENNYSON.
BORN
AUGUST 6 1809.
DIED
OCTOBER 6 1892

ROBERT
BROWNIN

MAYFAIR

Sitting between Oxford Street, Regent Street, Piccadilly and Park Lane, Mayfair is one of London's most affluent areas, dominated by luxurious offices and elegant Georgian housing. Only the wealthiest writers have lived here, including Lord Byron in 1814, and twentieth century novelists J. B. Priestly, Aldous Huxley and Graham Greene.

Tyburn Tree

Marble Arch was designed in 1827 as a triumphant arch in celebration of British victories in the Napoleonic Wars and as a magnificent gateway to an expanded Buckingham Palace. It was relocated in 1851, to the North East corner of Hyde Park, at Cumberland Gate. Marble Arch is mentioned in Oscar Wilde's *A Picture of Dorian Grey* (1890). Lord Henry is out walking and notices by the arch, 'a little crowd of shabby-looking people listening to some vulgar street-preacher'.

Marble Arch is close to the spot where Tyburn Gallows were used for public executions, until they moved to Newgate Prison in 1783. Dickens wrote about the

Marble Arch. Petr Kovalenkov/shutterstock.com

The Plaque commemorating the spot where London's accused were once hanged on Tyburn Tree.
Chrisdorney/shutterstock.com

Mayfair's Literary Gentlemen

William Blake lived on 17 South Molton Street with his wife Catherine between 1807 and 1827. During this time, frustrated that his work was failing to attract big sales and commissions, Blake slipped into paranoia and the couple fell into poverty. Blake died in 1827, shortly after leaving the house. The house is the only one of Blake's London homes still standing. The Blake Society are based at nearby St James' Church, Piccadilly, where they hold talks and events.

In Bram Stoker's *Dracula* (1897), Johnathan Harker, the solicitor and first to fall under Dracula's evil spell, sees the blood-sucking Count walking along Piccadilly, a couple of months after being rescued from his terrifying castle in Transylvania. Harker discovers, to his horror, that Dracula has bought a house at number 347. House numbers on the

overuse of hangings in the late eighteenth century in the preface to *Barnaby Rudge* (1841), highlighting the case of a Mary Jones, a teenage mother who was hanged at Tyburn for stealing linen, even though she had returned the cloth. Seventeenth century writers often approached those about to be hanged to ask for any writings they may have, to be published as memoirs or last confessions. The condemned would advertise their coming works to the crowds who assembled to watch the hangings. Jake Arnott's *The Fatal Tree* (2017), set in the underworld of eighteenth-century London, tells the story of lives changed and lost in the city's gaols, molly, ale and gin houses and on Tyburn Tree.

The plaque commemorating the only one of William Blake's London houses still standing, at 17 South Molton Street.

THE CORPORATION OF
WILLIAM BLAKE
POET & PAINTER
LIVED HERE
♦ BORN 1757 ♦
♦ DIED 1827 ♦
THE CITY OF LONDON

real Piccadilly do not reach 347 and Stoker's inspiration is believed to be number 138, opposite Green Park.

Next to the Hard Rock Café.

Perhaps the best-known Mayfair gentleman in fiction is P. G. Wodehouse's Bertie Wooster, in the *Jeeves Series* (1915–1974). Wooster lives at 3a Berkeley Mansions on Berkeley Square and can often be found at the nearby Drones Club, based on 'Bucks Club' at 18 Clifford Street, a private members club where 'Bucks Fizz' was invented. Wodehouse lived at 17 Dunraven Street (formally

Dunraven Street, once home to P. G. Wodehouse.
Phaustou/shutterstock.com

Norfolk Street) between 1927 and 1934. He published ten novels during that time.

Another famous Mayfair club was

The Hard Rock Café, with Eon House next door at 138, believed to be where Dracula lived in Bram Stoker's novel. Christian Storto/ shutterstock.com

the Albemarle Club at 37 Dover Street, now the art gallery, Ely House. This was where the Marquess of Queensbury left his calling card, 'For Oscar Wilde – posing Somdomite', in February 1895, leading to the libel case and Wilde's prosecution.

Mayfair's Literary Ladies

The prolific romantic novelist Barbara Cartland lived at various Mayfair addresses, including Half Moon Street, after separating from her husband. One of her 723 books was *Virgin in Mayfair* (1932), a thinly veiled autobiographical tale of a young debutante's experiences in London Society. Fifty years after it was published, Cartland admitted that the clubs, homes, events and most of the people in the book were real.

In Evelyn Waugh's novel *Vile Bodies* (1930), Mayfair's 'Bright Young Things' indulge in parties, heavy drinking and promiscuous sex, masking their vulnerabilities caused by the horrors of the First World War.

Mayfair's Barbara Cartland. B.Cat/shutterstock.com

MARYLEBONE

On the north side of Oxford Street, Marylebone is an elegant district of Georgian terraces.

Sherlock Holmes and 221b Baker Street

Amidst Marylebone's elegant town houses and shops is literature's most famous address, 221b Baker Street, the home of Sherlock Holmes and Dr Watson.

In Conan Doyle's first Holmes story *A Study in Scarlet* (1887), Watson is told, by a hospital colleague, of a man looking for someone to go halves in some nice rooms he has found for rent. This turns out to be the detective, Sherlock Holmes. Watson, at a loose end himself, agrees to move into Baker Street, and

Sherlock Holmes Museum.
LTerlecka/shutterstock.com

the adventures begin, adventures that would fill fifty-six short stories and four novels, spanning between 1887 and 1927, with scenes and episodes located all over London.

In Conan Doyle's time, Baker Street only went up to 85. Number 221b was added during an extension in 1930, but demolished soon afterwards to make space for Abbey House, the headquarters of the Abbey National Bank and Building Society. During the 1951 Festival of Britain, the house held a Holmes exhibition, including a reconstruction of the 221b sitting room as described in the books. This can now be found in the Sherlock Holmes pub off Charing Cross. The Building Society received forty letters a month addressed to the famous detective. Abbey House is now flats, and the post now goes to the Sherlock Holmes Museum, a few doors away at 237–241 Baker Street but with 221b on its door.

Sherlock Holmes statue at Baker Street Tube Station.
Yuri Turkov/shutterstock.com

Charles Dickens

Charles Dickens lived at 1 Devonshire Terrace, now 15 Marylebone Road, in 1839. His family was growing, and his first novels had been successful enough for him to move into one of Marylebone's sizable homes. The Dickens family grew by six during their time here and Charles wrote *The Old Curiosity Shop* (1841), *American Notes* (1842), *A Christmas Carol* (1843), *Martin Chuzzlewit* (1844), *Dombey and Son* (1848), and began *David Copperfield* (1850).

Dickens' close friend Wilkie Collins lived close by, at 65 Gloucester Palace, with a widow, Caroline and her daughter Harriett. Harriett scribed for Collins when his eyesight began to fail through overuse of opium and laudanum. Collins met Martha,

Wilkie Collins.
Morphart Creation/shutterstock.co

The site of Charles Dickens' house at 1 Devonshire Terrace is now occupied by Ferguson House. A relief mural on the side of the offices depicts some of Dickens' most famous characters. Chrisdorney/shutterstock.com

a nineteen-year-old, who moved to London to be close to him, and had three children with her, whilst continuing to live with Caroline and Harriett.

Elizabeth Barrett-Browning

The Victorian poet Elizabeth Barrett-Browning lived at 50 Wimpole Street, where she spent most of her time confined to her room with illness. She wrote her collection *Poems*

St Marylebone Church, where Elizabeth and Robert Browning were married in secret in 1909.
Dreamcatcher Diana/shutterstock.com

(1908) here. In 1909, she met Robert Browning, a great fan of her work, who visited her over 90 times. Elizabeth's father disapproved of her courting and the couple married in secret at St Marylebone Church, Marylebone Road. This was the first time the couple had met outside the ailing writer's home. Elizabeth fainted on the way to church and was bought round with smelling salts. Her father never forgave her. A week later, the couple eloped to Italy. Rudolph Besier sympathetically retold the story in his play, *The Barretts of Wimpole Street* (1930).

Almost sixty years before the Brownings began their clandestine relationship, Wimpole Street was the setting of Tennyson's poem of grief and loss, *In Memoriam* (1850). Tennyson describes the street as 'long' and 'unlovely' after the death of his friend, Arthur Hallam, who had lived there. Wilkie Collins died at number 82 Wimpole Street in 1889.

In George Bernard Shaw's *Pygmalion* (1913), retold in the more famous musical and film *My Fair Lady*, Professor Higgins lives at 27A Wimpole Street.

Heywood Hill Bookshop, 10 Curzon Street

The author Nancy Mitford worked as an assistant here during the Second World War. Her gregarious and witty nature was popular with customers, helping establish the shop as a centre of

London's social and literary life. Evelyn Waugh claimed the shop in Mitford's time was, 'a centre for all that was left of fashionable and intellectual London.' Mitford left the shop in 1945, following the successful publication of her first novel, *The Pursuit of Love*. Heywood Hill still maintains delightful personal touches with handwritten receipts and books beautifully wrapped in brown paper.

Hatchards, 187 Piccadilly

Eighteen-year-old Noël Coward once walked into this shop with a suitcase he had stolen from next door Fortnum and Mason, and started filling it with books. When apprehended by an assistant he snapped that the bookshop was so badly run he could have made off with the books without anyone noticing, and left.

Hatchards Piccadilly, the oldest bookshop in London opened in 1797. Olivier Guilberteau/shutterstock.com

FITZROVIA

Fitzrovia is a tightly populated and diverse area of London, with grand eighteenth and nineteenth century apartments sitting side-by-side with social housing.

Fitzrovia's Writers

Fitzrovia was Charles Dickens' first London home. The family moved to 22 Cleveland Street in 1816, when his father got work as a clerk at Somerset House on the Strand.

George Bernard Shaw lived at 29 Fitzroy Square from 1887 to 1898, where he wrote many plays, including *Mrs*

Number 29 Fitzroy Square was lived in by George Bernard Shaw and, later, Virginia Woolf.
Spiroview Inc/shutterstock.com

Warren's Profession (1893) and *Caesar and Cleopatra* (1898). He left the house to marry Charlotte Payne-Townshend, who was shocked when she visited him here to find he worked in a very small room, 'in a perpetual state of dirt and disorder'. A decade later, Virginia Woolf (then Virginia Stephen) moved into the house with her brother Adrian.

Doris Lessing lived in Holbein Mansions, 25 Langham Street, in the late 1950s in a flat she rented from her publisher for £5 a week. Here she wrote her classic, *A Golden Notebook* (1962). Doris hosted international envoys for

Nobel Prize for Literature and multi-award winner, Doris Lessing was one of the world's most respected writers and an avid campaigner for anti-racism and communism. Mario Breda/shutterstock.com

the new British Left and held political gatherings in her flat. The American Diplomat, Henry Kissinger, once paid her a visit, wanting to meet members of the Campaign for Nuclear Disarmament who met here. Lessing later recalled the 'crew-cut, prosperous American' seemed too 'fresh and glistening' for her dingy flat. In 2015, nearly two years after her death, The National Archives published a five-volume file that MI5 and MI6 had built up on Lessing. These revealed that her passionate campaigning for communism and anti-racism had come to the attention of the British intelligence Agencies in the early 1940s, who had then placed her under surveillance for twenty years.

Broadcasting House

Fitzrovia is the home of the BBC. Broadcasting House, its headquarters, stands on the corner of Portland Place and Langham Place. Ever since the BBC made its first radio broadcast, on 15 March, 1932, London's writers have found work here, and the famous Art Deco building has been the inspiration for some of their best known scenes. Dylan Thomas was commissioned to broadcast live poetry readings in the 1940s. Once after a little too much whisky, he was found fast asleep and snoring into the microphone. The shock of being woken by his producer sobered Thomas enough to deliver his reading with just a few slurred words. Penelope Fitzgerald drew on her wartime experiences working at

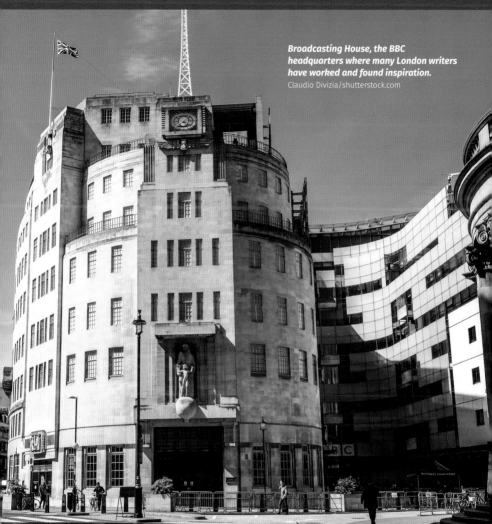

Broadcasting House, the BBC headquarters where many London writers have worked and found inspiration.
Claudio Divizia/shutterstock.com

Broadcasting House in *Human Voices* (1980), a satire of life working in the BBC during the Second World War.

The most famous depiction of Broadcasting House in fiction is as 'Room 101' in George Orwell's *1984* (1949). Bloomsbury's Senate House was the inspiration for 'The Ministry of Truth', but its Room 101 was named after a room where Orwell had to endure tedious meetings when he worked for the BBC during the Second World War. The Ministry of Truth's canteen was inspired by the canteen here, dismal

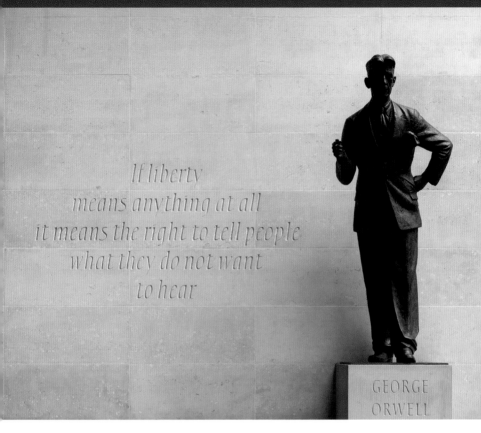

If liberty
means anything at all
it means the right to tell people
what they do not want
to hear

GEORGE
ORWELL

A striking bronze statue of George Orwell was unveiled outside Broadcasting House in 2017.
Claudio Divizia/shutterstock.com

with no window. The dinner ladies wheeling coffee for tired journalists are recreated in the novel.

The Langham Hotel, Portland Place

Just around the corner from Broadcasting House is the luxurious Langham Hotel. Oscar Wilde and Arthur Conan Doyle were invited to meet an American agent, Joseph Stoddart, here in August 1889. It turned out to be a pivotal moment for both writers. Stoddart commissioned Wilde to write his only novel, *The Pictures of Dorian Grey* (1890). Conan Doyle had published the first of his Holmes stories, *A Study in Scarlet* (1887), and wanted to turn his attention to historical romances. Stoddart persuaded him to write another detective story and Conan Doyle took on his first Holmes commission, the novella *The Sign of Four* (1890).

Fitzrovia's Pubs and Hotels

In its mid-twentieth century Bohemian heyday, Fitzrovia's literary scene revolved around its pubs, where local writers who didn't fit in with the stiffer Bloomsbury Group formed into more relaxed groupings.

The Fitzroy Tavern, 16 Charlotte Street

In the early twentieth century, this gaudy Victorian pub was the centre of Bohemian Fitzrovia, drawing artists and writers such as Dylan Thomas, artists and politicians to gather around its honky-tonk piano. The arts crowd moved to the nearby Wheatsheaf when the pub became more mainstream and touristy in the mid 1900s

The Wheatsheaf, 25 Rathbone Place

Now a members' club, 'One Percy Street' was once The Eiffel Tower Hotel, home to 'The Poets' Club' in the early 1900s and frequented by Aldous Huxley,

The Weatsheaf on Rathbone Place is a favourite pub for London's writers. CK Travels/shutterstock.com

Evelyn Waugh and George Bernard Shaw. The painter Augustus John began an affair here with a young Irish girl, Caitlin Macnamara, who had run away to London to become a dancer. John introduced Caitlin to Dylan Thomas at The Wheatsheaf in April 1936 and the poet fell in love with her at first sight. They spent the next six days at the Eiffel Tower Hotel, leaving the bill to be picked up by John. Dylan and Caitlin married and lodged near their favourite Fitzrovia and Soho pubs, before finally moving to their home in Camden. George Orwell, Edwin Muir and Humphrey Jennings also drank here at the time. Together with Thomas, they were known as the 'Wheatsheaf Writers'. Nina Hamnet, Quentin Crisp, Anthony Burgess and Russel Brand are among others who have visited the Wheatsheaf, a pub that remains popular with writers.

Duke of York, 47 Rathborne Street

In 1943, Anthony Burgess was here having a drink with his wife, Lynne, when a gang armed with razor blades stormed in, demanded several pints then poured the beer, smashed the glasses on the wall and began brandishing broken glass at terrified customers. Lynne was not so scared by the incident, saying later the gang reminded her of Pinkie's gang in Graham Greene's *Brighton Rock* (1938). When she protested the gang had wasted good beer, their leader pulled her several pints and ordered her to drink them. Lynne downed the lot and he was so impressed he handed her money to the value of all she had drunk and offered the couple protection from other local gangs. Burgess used the experience as inspiration for 'The Droogs' in *A Clockwork Orange* (1962).

2

NORTH WEST LONDON

CAMDEN

The Borough of Camden rests just on the north east edge of Central London, stretching from Holborn to Highgate. Camden Town itself is known for its canal-side market, alternative clothing, record shops and music venues.

The Home of the Cratchits

Ten-year-old Charles Dickens lived at 141 Bayham Gardens with his family between 1822 and 1823. Camden Town was a rustic town then, with haymaking in the meadows at the back of the family home. Although he was only here a year before the family moved to Bloomsbury, this 'shabby, dingy, damp and mean neighbourhood' made a lasting impression on Dickens, who later depicted the house as the Cratchits' home, where Christmas is celebrated in *A Christmas Carol* (1843), then Mr Micawber's house in *David Copperfield* (1850).

The Cratchits' home in A Christmas Carol (1843) was inspired by Dickens' childhood home in Bayham Gardens, Camden. Dave Rheaume Artist/shutterstock.com

St Pancras Church Graveyard, Somers Town

In *A Tale of Two Cities* (1859) the resurrection men steal corpses from the graves at St Pancras Old Church to sell to London's medical students to dissect. A few years later, in the mid 1860s, while studying architecture under Arthur Blomfield, Thomas Hardy was put in charge of excavating part of the graveyard to make way for St Pancras Station being built nearby.

The Hardy Tree in the churchyard of St Pancras Old Church, circled by gravestones placed there by the writer, Thomas Hardy. AC Manley/shutterstock.com

The job involved moving an ancient Ash tree, and 'The Hardy Tree' can be seen growing between the gravestones he stacked up when moving them to the smaller churchyard.

Mary Wollstonecraft Godwin first told Percy Bysshe Shelley she loved him over her mother, Mary Wollstonecraft's, grave at St Pancras Old Church. Mary Wollstonecraft died a few days after her daughter was born from complications during childbirth.

The Boy Who Lived

Kings Cross Station has become famous for 'Platform 9¾', where Harry Potter and his friends catch the Hogwarts Express to school. In the first book, *Harry Potter and the Philosopher's Stone* (1997), Harry meets the Weasley family at the station, who explain Platform 9¾

Potter fans can find a statue of a loaded school trolley in the wall between Kings Cross platforms 9 and 10, where they can pose for photos and pretend to be entering the magical platform. Richart Photos/shutterstock.com

is a portal from the muggle station into the wizarding world and can only be

A bronze statue of Sir John Betjeman looking up at the magnificent architecture he helped save.
chrisdorney/shutterstock.com

home to the world's biggest collection of literature, holding over fourteen million books and manuscripts dating back as far as 2000BC, many of which are on public display in its exhibitions. Here you can see original manuscripts, including: *Beowulf* (c.975–1025), Shakespeare's first folio, Chaucer's *The Canterbury Tales* (1392), Jane Austen's *Persuasion* (1817), Dickens' *Nicolas Nickleby* (1839), Charlotte Brontë's *Jane Eyre* (1847) and Virginia Woolf's *Mrs Dalloway* (1925). Alongside the permanent exhibits, the library hosts frequent thematic exhibitions that vary from children's literature favourites to magical and sacred texts and the history of the English language.

Kings Cross is the setting of Olumide Popoola's 2017 novel, *When We Speak of Nothing,* that follows best friends, Karl

reached by running into the wall between platforms nine and ten. J. K. Rowling chose Kings Cross station because her parents met here, on a train to Scotland, and she held happy memories travelling from here as a child.

Sir John Betjeman was a train enthusiast and a passionate defender of Victorian architecture. A bronze statue of the poet stands at the concourse of St Pancras Station in recognition for his efforts in helping save it from demolition.

The British Library

The British Library moved from The British Museum to 96 Euston Road, near Kings Cross St Pancras Station, in 1973. It is

The entrance to the British Library on Euston Road.
Lucian Milasan/shutterstock.com

and Abdu through a story set against the London riots that followed Mark Duggan's shooting by police in 2011. In an early scene, the contrast between the big estates in Kings Cross and the 'pretty' areas of Regents Street and Bloomsbury is shown through Abdu's eyes on his fifteen-minute walk to sixth-form college.

Camden Town

Dylan Thomas, his wife Caitlin, and their three children moved to 54 Delancey Street, at the heart of Camden Town, in 1950, after a wealthy patron of Dylan's, Mary Taylor, bought them the apartment in an attempt to keep them in London. Her plan didn't work. Dylan toured America the next year and never returned, calling it his 'London House of Horror'.

The playwright Alan Bennett lived at 23 Gloucester Crescent for forty years. *The Lady in the Van* (1990) tells the real-life story of Miss Shephard, a homeless lady who lived in a van in Bennett's driveway from 1974 until her death in 1989. The house was used in the film, after which Bennett sold it for three million pounds and moved to nearby Primrose Hill.

Harold Pinter lived at 38 Burghley Road, at nearby Kentish Town, from 1962–1969, whilst having the secret affair with journalist and broadcaster, Joan Bakewell, that inspired his play, *Betrayal* (1978).

The colour and excitement of modern-day Camden Town is portrayed as a contrast to the north of England in David Storey's *Flight into Camden* (1961), and as the back drop for eighteen-year-old Eily's affair with the older, handsome but damaged actor, Stephen, in Eimear McBride's *The Lesser Bohemians* (2016).

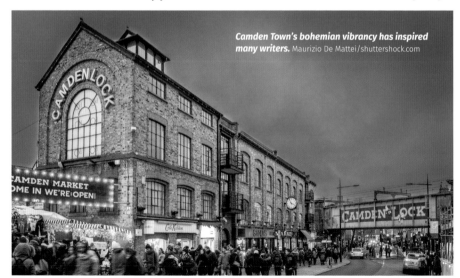

Camden Town's bohemian vibrancy has inspired many writers. Maurizio De Mattei/shuttershock.com

REGENTS PARK

Just north-west of Central London is Regents Park, the Royal Park and home to London Zoo.

Potter fans often arrive here to see the reptile house, where Harry first realises he is a 'parselmouth' and able to speak the snake language. While the zoo was used to film the scene in the movie, *Harry Potter and the Philosopher's Stone*, it is not the zoo in J. K. Rowling's 1997 book, where Harry later tells Hagrid, during their shopping trip, that he has never been to London before. The zoo is featured in Russel Hoban's poignant novel, *Turtle Diary* (1975), where two lonely London misfits strike a friendship when visiting the sea turtles. The book

was adapted by Harold Pinter for the 1985 film.

In 1914, the zoo was given Winnipeg, a black bear and mascot of a Canadian regiment that had been called to the trenches. The zoo was a favourite outing for A. A. Milne and his son, Christopher Robin, and Milne used to tell Christopher stories about Winnipeg – Winnie-the Pooh.

Regents Park's rose-gardens in Queen Mary's Gardens are beautifully portrayed when the middle-aged gardening enthusiast Myra arrives to take cuttings and rekindles the relationship

Winnie-the-Pooh was inspired by visits to London Zoo, Regents Park. Steve Mann/shutterstock.com

Queen Mary's Rose Gardens in Regents Park. chrisdorney/shutterstock.com

The lake in Regent's Park where Marcus accidentally kills a duck with his mother's home-baked bread in Nick Hornby's **About a Boy** *(1998).*
LanaG/shutterstock.com

with her estranged daughter in *Among the Roses*, in Doris Lessing's *London Observed* (1992), a wondrous book of stories and sketches set all over the city.

The park is also where Nick Hornby placed the scene for the famous 'dead duck day' in his novel and film *About a Boy* (1998 and 2002).

PRIMROSE HILL

Primrose Hill is a fashionable residential area. The hill itself is a popular place to relax, exercise and look over central London.

In H. G. Wells' *The Invisible Man* (1897), Griffin sits at the top of the hill on a sunny day, thinking about how he has made a cat disappear, before going back to his lodgings on Great Portland Street and making himself invisible. A year later, in Wells' *War of the Worlds* (1898) the Martians attempt to make the hill their headquarters during their attack on London. Aldous Huxley refers to the anti-aircraft guns situated at the top of Primrose Hill during the Second World War in his novel *Time Must Have a Stop* (1944). Helen Falconer's novel, *Primrose Hill* (1999), follows a group of adolescents hanging out on the hill over the summer, though all is not as idyllic in their lives in the city below. Perhaps

Primrose Hill is a popular setting for London's writers.
lazyllama/shutterstock.com

the best loved characters seen on Primrose Hill are Pongo and Missus and their canine friends who escaped up the hill from Regents Park in Dodie Smith's *101 Dalmatians* (1956), the book behind the famous Disney film.

Sylvia Plath and Ted Hughes

Ted Hughes and Sylvia Plath moved into a small one-bedroomed flat at 3 Chalcot Square, at the bottom of Primrose Hill, in 1960. Plath wrote her autobiographical novel *The Bell Jar* (1963) here before their marriage dissolved and she moved, with their two young children, around the corner to 23 Fitzroy Road in 1962.

Plath worked from four am each morning, battling her growing depression, to complete her collection, *Ariel* (1965). The collection included *Lady Lazarus*, where Plath reflects on her obsession with death and her regular attempts to end her own life. On 1 February 1963, the troubled poet put her children to bed and finally succeeded in ending her life by gassing herself with the cooker.

Olga Popoua/shutterstock.com

Plath said the house at 23 Fitzroy Road was a house she always wanted to live at: 'It is W. B. Yeats' house with a blue plaque above the door saying he lived here'.

HAMPSTEAD HEATH

The picturesque and stylish Hampstead Heath is one of London's key literary and intellectual centres, where many of its most affluent writers have lived over the years. Robert Louis Stephenson, who lived here for a month in 1874, said Hampstead was 'the most delightful place for air and scenery in London'. In her 1922 diary, Virginia Woolf acknowledged Hampstead as 'the heart of the enemies' camp', due to discord between its literary scene and her Bloomsbury group.

Keats Grove

John Keats moved to Hampstead with his brothers in 1817. Their house at 1 Well Walk, now Keats Grove, was close to the homes of other poets in his circle, including Leigh Hunt and Samuel Taylor Coleridge.

Well Walk was renamed Keats Grove in honour of its famous former resident. phaustov/shuttershock.com

Keats wrote one of his best loved poems, *Ode to a Nightingale* (1819), under a plum tree in his garden after hearing a bird while he was having a drink at nearby Spaniard's Inn. It was here Keats fell in love with Fanny Brawne, and where he developed his first symptoms of tuberculosis, the disease that led to his death in 1821, at

Keats House is open to the public as a museum dedicated to the poet. Victoria Allum/shuttershock.com

The plaque acknowledging Joanna Baillie's fifty years at Bolton House was one of the first to be awarded to a woman. waymarking.com

just twenty-five years old.

Keats' friend Leigh Hunt lived at Vale Lodge, Vale of Heath, from 1815, after his release from prison where he was being held for libel. While living in Hampstead he formed the 'Hunt Circle', with poets including Keats, Shelley, Lord Byron and Charles Lamb.

The celebrated poet and playwright, Joanna Baillie, lived with her sister for fifty years at Bolton House, Windmill Hill during the early nineteenth century. Baille hosted London's first literary salon here, with Keats, Wordsworth and Byron among those who attended.

Orwell's Hampstead

In the 1920s George Orwell often visited friends at 1B Oakwood Road, where he would dress as a tramp and set off to spend time with those sleeping rough in London's East End and Embankment. It was here Orwell wrote the first draft of his memoir about life in poverty among them, *Down and out in Paris and London* (1931). From 1934 to 1937, Orwell lived at 37 Pond Street, in a flat above a second-hand bookshop called Booklover's Corner. Orwell worked part time here to supplement his writing income. During his time here, Orwell grew a loathing of the bourgeois socialists who lived around him. He attacked them savagely in *The Road to Wigan Pier* (1937). *Keep the Aspidistra Flying* (1936), a satire on society's preoccupation with money, was set mostly in Hampstead.

Daphne Du Maurier

Daphne Du Maurier lived at Canon Hall, 14 Cannon Place, in 1916, when she was nine years old. Her father, Sir Gerald, was a leading actor and played Captain Cook in the first production of J. M. Barrie's *Peter Pan*. In 2015, the mansion, regarded as one of London's finest homes, sold for twenty-four million pounds.

D. H. Lawrence

D. H. Lawrence and his wife moved to Vale of Heath's 1 Byron Villas, where he wrote and published *The Rainbow* (1915). Lawrence was not happy in Hampstead and the couple moved to Cornwall, where locals thought his wife, Frieda, to be a German spy and they were forced to move back to London.

Admiral's Walk

Admiral's House is curious house on Admiral's Walk, with a roof resembling a ship's quarterdeck. This was the inspiration for Admiral Boom's house in P. L. Travers' *Mary Poppins* (1934). Grove Lodge, the only other house in Admiral's walk, was home to John Galsworthy between 1918 and 1933, where he wrote the ending of *Forsyte Saga* (1922). In 1932 Galsworthy was awarded the Nobel Prize for Literature but was too ill to collect it, so a delegation arrived to deliver it. He died here soon afterwards.

Grove Lodge, where John Galsworthy lived his last years and was awarded his Nobel Prize.
Paul Wishart/shuttershock

Agatha Christie

Agatha Christie moved to Iskonon Flats on Lawn Road, after her Kensington flat was damaged in the Blitz. Members of the 'Cambridge Spy Ring', who passed information to the Soviets during the Second World War and subsequent Cold War, lived here at the same time.

Hampstead Heath in Fiction

C. S. Lewis was inspired with the idea for *The Lion, the Witch and the Wardrobe* (1850) during a snowy afternoon walk on Hampstead Heath.

Other writers have found inspiration in the heath's darker, lonelier more

Hampstead Heath was the inspiration for C. S. Lewis' magical world, Narnia, in The Lion the Witch and the Wardrobe (1850). photocritical/shutterstock.com

desolate side. In *Barnaby Rudge* (1841), Dickens writes of eighteenth-century robbers so violent that few would venture into Hampstead 'unarmed and unattended'.

Lucy Westenra lived and was buried in Hampstead in Bram Stoker's *Dracula* (1897). When she rises as a vampire, Lucy abducts children who are later found on the heath, dead with punctured throats.

George Smiley finds the corpse of the old White Russian on the heath, in John Le Carre's *Smiley's People* (1979). The opening scenes of Wilkie Collins' *The Woman in White* (1859) are set on Hampstead Heath, where Walter Hartright first encounters the strange, spooky woman. Hampstead is the setting

The graves at St John-at-Hampstead inspired Bram Stoker in creating his vampire, Dracula (1897). The novel's Lucy Westenra is buried here.
photocritical/shutterstock.com

for Will Self's *The Book of Dave* (2006), and Zadie Smith wrote about the area in *On Beauty* (2005) and *NW* (2012).

Zadie Smith was born in nearby Willesden and went to Hampstead School on Westbere Road. Zadie has used her home borough as the backdrop for her most famous novels. *White Teeth* (2000) is set in Willesden and Kilburn between 1972 and 1992. The story of the two wartime friends, Samad Iqbal and Archie Jones, and their London families is beautifully told against the backdrop of multicultural, working class Greater London.

The Spaniard's Inn, Spaniard's Road

This iconic cosy pub is where Keats heard the Nightingale that inspired his famous poem. In *Barnaby Rudge* (1841), the Gordon Rioters stop off here on their way to Lord Mansfield's House but they are stalled by the landlord who sends for the army and prevents the raid. The pub also features in Bram Stoker's *Dracula* (1897) when Dr John Stewart comes here after visiting Lucy's tomb.

The Old Bull and Bush, North End Road

This luxurious pub, opposite Golders Hill Park in North Hampstead, made famous by the 1903 music-hall song, 'Down at the Old Bull and Bush', was a favourite of writers, including Charles Dickens. This is also where Charles Pooter and his friends drink after their Sunday walk across the Heath in George and Weedon Grossmith's *The Diary of a Nobody* (1892).

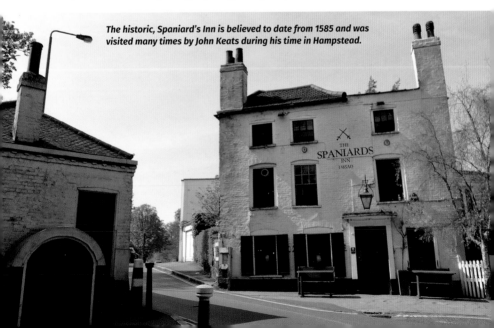

The historic, Spaniard's Inn is believed to date from 1585 and was visited many times by John Keats during his time in Hampstead.

The White Horse, 154 Fleet Road

Comstock wishes he was be able to afford a drink here in Orwell's *Keep the Aspidistra Flying* (1936). Owners planned to remove the pub's clock in the 1980s, but local residents were successful in campaigning for it to stay in honour of it being mentioned in the novel.

Kentish Town

John Betjeman was born in 1906 at Parliament Hill Mansions, Lissendsen Gardens, Kentish Town. Betjeman was never fond of the area but was always pleased to have been born within a few hundred yards of a station, Gospel Oak, on his favourite railway, the new Northern Line.

ST JOHN'S WOOD

George Orwell and H. G. Wells

In 1940, George Orwell and his wife lived in a flat above H. G. Wells' garage on Hanover Terrace, near Regents Park. Wells believed Orwell had been gossiping about him and demanded they moved out. In an attempt to patch things up, Orwell invited Wells to dinner at his new address at 111 Lanfort Court, St John's Wood. Wells accepted but, strangely, asked Orwell why he had left his flat so suddenly. At the dinner party, Wells told the Orwells he had some tummy trouble and wouldn't be able to eat, then helped himself to two portions of curry and some plum cake. A week later, he wrote to his hosts, 'You knew I was ill and

A plaque marks the spot where George and Eileen Orwell's house once stood on Mortimer Crescent.
chrisdorney/shuttershock.com

on a diet and you deliberately plied me with food and drink. I never want to see you again.' He never did!

The Orwells later lived nearby in West Hampstead, at 10a Mortimer Crescent. In June 1944 a V1 flying bomb landed in the street, causing their ceiling to collapse. The only manuscript for his novel *Animal Farm* (1945) ended up amongst the rubble. Thankfully, the couple found it still legible. The house has since been demolished.

A. A. Milne and H. G. Wells

A. A. Milne's father ran Henley House School, a small school in St John's Wood, between 1893 and 1900 where, in 1889, the young author was taught science by a youthful teacher called H. G. Wells.

Doris Lessing

After writing more than fifty novels, the much-loved Nobel Prize winner, Doris Lessing, died in 2013 at 24 Gondar Gardens, West Hampstead, at the age of ninety-four.

3

NORTH LONDON

ISLINGTON

Islington was a slum throughout the Victorian era and much of the twentieth century. The area gained desirability after the Victoria Line opened in 1970 and is now a fashionable residential area of North London.

In Neil Gaiman's fantasy novel *Neverwhere* (1996), The Angel Islington is a real angel who lives in the sewers of London and watches over 'London Below', a magical realm that co-exists with the more familiar 'London Above'.

The Angel, Islington, refers to the corner of Islington High Street and Pentonville Road, where The Angel Inn stood from 1614. Peter Moulton/shuttershock.com

Joe Orton and Kenneth Halliwell

Playwright Joe Orton and his lover, the artist Kenneth Halliwell, lived at 25 Noel Road, close to the Angel, in 1959, long before Islington grew in popularity. The pair spent much of the early 1960s in Islington Library, creating 'guerilla art': defacing books by inserting text and creating alternative covers, in reaction to the 'endless shelves of rubbish' they found there. Suspicious staff were told by police they would need to find proof in a letter confirming the perpetrators' identities. A determined librarian faked a council note, threatening to remove one of the couple's clapped out cars. Halliwell responded with a letter typed on the same machine the pair had used

Islington Central Library, 2 Fieldway Crescent Highbury, now has a Joe Orton collection, including many of the books and covers the pair refashioned. Julian Osley/geograph.org.uk

The house on Noel Road, where Joe Orton and Kenneth Halliwell lived before their violent and tragic deaths in 1967. Christopher Hilton/geograph.org.uk

for their pranks. The police searched their house on Noel Road and found hundreds of photos of their vandalised books plastered over the walls.

Orton and Halliwell were prosecuted and spent six months in Wormwood Scrubs. After release Orton wrote some of his best plays, including *Entertaining Mr Sloane* (1964) and *Loot* (1966), and became one of the most celebrated playwrights of the time.

In August 1967, Halliwell beat Orton to death during a row, before taking his own life. Twenty-years after the playwright's death, the unfettered diary he kept during the last year of his life at Noel Road was found. *The Orton Diaries* were edited by his biographer, John Lahr and published in 1986.

Canonbury

Further north into Islington is the area of Canonbury, where council estates stand amongst townhouses and late Georgian villas. George Orwell moved into number 27b Canonbury Square with Eileen in 1944, after they were bombed out of their home in St Johns. The Orwells enjoyed a happy time here. They adopted their only son and became known among their friends and colleagues for their sumptuous high teas, served with strong tea poured from a two-handled gallon-sized pot. A year after they arrived here, Eileen went under anaesthetic for a hysterectomy and never woke up. Orwell started work on *1984* (1949) here and based Victory

Canonbury Square, the inspiration for Victory Mansions in Orwell's 1984 (1949). Stephen McKay/ geograph.org.uk

having to explain to friends why he lived in such an appalling district.

Old Street Police Station and Magistrates Court

Over Christmas in 1932, Orwell deliberately set out to get drunk in Mile End, so he could be arrested and experience life in prison. He was convicted for being drunk and disorderly at Old Street Magistrates Court in nearby Hoxton and fined six shillings. In May 1962, Orton and Halliwell were charged here for stealing and defacing seventy-two library books from Islington Library. The couple were called, 'a malice towards fellow library users' by the judge who awarded them their six-month prison sentence

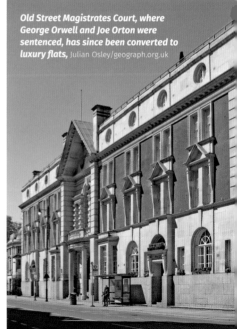

Old Street Magistrates Court, where George Orwell and Joe Orton were sentenced, has since been converted to luxury flats, Julian Osley/geograph.org.uk

Mansions, the home of Winston Smith, on Canonbury Gardens.

Evelyn Waugh moved into 17a Canonbury Square in 1928 with his first wife, Evelyn Gardener, one of the 'Bright Young Things' among bohemian aristocrats and socialites in 1920s London. The couple, known to friends as 'He-velyn and She-velyn', divorced after just over a year. Waugh wrote *Decline and Fall* (1928) here before he moved out, saying he had become bored of

HIGHGATE

Highgate was once a distinct village outside of London. It became an inner suburb with the advent of the railways. It is still surrounded by green, edging on the east of Hampstead Heath and with Highgate Wood to the north. This exclusive area has some of the most expensive housing in London.

Samuel Taylor Coleridge lived at 3, The Grove, with his physician, Dr James Gillman, who Coleridge hired to help him overcome his addiction to opium. Unfortunately, the drug was in good supply at the nearby Dunn's chemist at Townshend Yard. He wrote many volumes of poetry and prose here, including *Work Without Hope* (1825), where he reflects on his drug addiction. He died here in 1834 and is buried across the road at the Church of St Michael.

J. B. Priestley moved into the same house from 1932 to 1940, where he wrote many of his plays and novels, including *Let the People Sing* (1930).

The Flask, 77 Highgate West Hill

The Flask was a favourite among the romantic poets, Lord Byron, Keats and Shelley, when they visited Coleridge in Highgate.

Samuel Taylor Coleridge.
Everett Collection/shuttershock.com

Samuel Taylor Coleridge lived across the road from The Flask, a historic pub dating back to 1663.
CK Travels/shuttershock.com

Highgate Cemetery, Swains Lane

Many famous people are buried among Highgate Cemetery's 50,000 graves, including Karl Marx, George Eliot, Christina Rossetti, John Galsworthy, Douglas Adams, Charles Dickens' parents, and his wife, Catherine.

When Elizabeth Siddal, the poet and wife of Dante Gabriel Rossetti, died suddenly from laudanum poisoning in 1862, Rossetti buried a book of new poems with her. Seven years later, the impoverished poet arranged for the coffin to be exhumed so he could earn from his poems. Each page had to be soaked with disinfectant before it was in a fit state to be presented for publication.

Highgate Cemetery provides an atmospheric setting for Tracey Chevalier's historical novel, *Falling Angels* (2009), and Audrey Niffeneger's spooky *Her Fearful Symmetry* (2010).

Highgate Cemetery. Gary Perkin/shutterstock.com

HOLLOWAY AND HIGHBURY AND STOKE NEWINGTON

Holloway, Highbury and Stoke Newington sit on the north edges of Islington and Hackney. This area of London is diverse and cosmopolitan, with multicultural shops and residences.

Diary of a Nobody and a Somebody

Holloway is the setting for George and Weedon Grossmith's *Diary of a Nobody* (1892). Charles Pooter and his family lived in 'Laurels, Brickfield Terrace' at One Pemberton Gardens. The house has since been converted into flats.

Joe Orton used to cruise along Holloway Road in the 1960s, looking for casual sex. In March 1967, shortly before being murdered by Halliwell, Orton entered a public urinal under the rail bridge on Holloway Road for a frenzied orgy with seven men, while passers-by carried on their ordinary business around them. In a nod to Grossmiths' book, he headed this entry 'Diary of a Somebody' in his diary *The Orton Diaries* (1986).

Douglas Adams lived in 19 Kingsdown Road in 1978, where he wrote *The Hitchhiker's Guide to the Galaxy* (1981)

Daniel Defoe

Daniel Defoe lived at 95 Church Street in Stoke Newington from 1708–1730. Despite being in his fifties, he started writing novels here and wrote *Robinson Crusoe* (1719), *Moll Flanders* (1722) and *A Journal of the Plague Year* (1722). In 1730, at nearly seventy, he fled from enemies and went into hiding in the City, where he died on Ropemaker Street.

Holloway and Stoke Newington in Fiction

Irvine Welsh lived in Stoke Newington for many years and wrote *Stoke Newington Blues* (1995) about its drug scene. Church Street, Stoke Newington is is where Mark Renton has a homosexual encounter with the waiter, Gi, in Welsh's *Trainspotting* (1993). Harold Pinter was born and educated in nearby Hackney in 1930 and set his semi-autobiographical novel *The Dwarfs* (1963) here. Nick Hornby's autobiographical book, *Fever Pitch* (1992), tells the story of his obsession with Arsenal, with poignant and amusing tales of a life often centering around the famous Highbury pitch.

The bridge where Joe Orton enjoyed an orgy in a 'little pissoir'. The toilets have since been boarded up. Rory Mccrea/shutterstock.com

4

EAST LONDON

THE EAST END AND DOCKLANDS

The East End of London is an area that has been shaped by poverty, prostitution, drugs and violence. Over the centuries it has been the destination of immigrants, arriving by boat to the East End docks, looking for a better life, often fleeing from persecution.

East End Docks

Michael Sadler's novel, *Fanny by Gaslight* (1947), tells the story of Victorian prostitution, when girls were bought over from West End brothels to serve the growing number of men working on the docks and ships.

Arthur Morrison was born in Poplar in 1863, and in *A Child of Jago* (1896) he follows a young boy through his descent into crime in Jago, a terrifying slum near Shoreditch Church on Old Nichol Street. The midwife, Jennifer Worth, wrote about her experiences working as a community nurse and midwife during the impoverished Poplar of the 1950s in *Call the Midwife* (2002). Worth's trilogy was closely followed in the first three

Modern-day Poplar with luxury office blocks standing neck-to-neck with high rise social housing. BillyDoogs/shutershock.com

Many a tale has been shared at G. Kelly's Pie and Mash Shop, 526 Roman Road, which has been run by the same family for over 100 years.

series of the popular TV series.

Melanie McGrath's *Pie and Mash down the Roman Road* (2018) is a biography of a long-standing pie and mash shop on one of London's last remaining traditional market roads. In *Silvertown* (2012) Melanie McGrath follows the life of her grandmother, Jenny Fulcher, born in Poplar in 1903, from her childhood in the deprived, but close-knit East End through the community disintegration that came with gentrification.

In *Life in Cockney London* (1999) Glinda O'Neil draws both on her memories, and the area's oral history, in her story about the hardships faced by dockland tug skippers.

Orwell's Ministry of Love

George Orwell spent a few hours at Bethnal Green Police Station after his arrest for being drunk and disorderly in 1931. His cell became the inspiration for the 'Ministry of Love' in *1984* (1949). Orwell spent his time counting porcelain bricks on the wall, as does Winston in the novel.

LIMEHOUSE AND ISLE OF DOGS

The original Chinatown

London's first Chinatown grew up here at the end of the nineteenth century, bringing new culture as well as noodle bars, opium dens and gambling dives to the area. In Oscar Wilde's *The Picture of Dorian Gray* (1890), Gray visits a Limehouse opium den to find the 'cure for the soul'. Thomas Burke was inspired to write his stories in *Limehouse Nights* (1916) after recalling a conversation he had with a Chinese man when he was six-years-old.

The opium and gambling dens of nineteenth century Limehouse have now been replaced with riverside flats and narrowboats. phaustov/shuttershock.com

Charles Dickens had a godfather who ran a chandler's shop on Garford Street and he mentions Limehouse in *Dombey and Sons* (1848) and *Our Mutual Friend* (1865).

The Grapes, 76 Narrow Street

The Grapes opened in 1720 and there has been a public house on this site since 1583. It features in Dickens' *Our Mutual Friend* (1865) under the name of 'The Six Jolly Fellowship Porters'. The pub commemorates its Dickensian links with sketches of his characters adorning the walls. The Grapes was also featured in Oscar Wilde's *The Picture of Dorian Gray* (1891).

WAPPING

Wapping was the site of the original London docks, active here until 1969. Geoffrey Chaucer worked here between 1374 and 1386 as a customs controller.

The Wapping Murders

In December 1811, a draper, his wife, baby and apprentice were gruesomely murdered in their house on 29 Ratcliff Highway. Twelve days later, a publican, his wife and maid were murdered at the Kings Arms, 81 New Gravel Lane. A sailor, John Williams, was accused and hung himself before he could be arrested. His body was paraded through the streets and a stake was driven through his heart for fear he could become a vampire. In his satirical essay, *Murder Considered as One of the Fine Arts* (1827) Thomas de Quincey describes the murders as 'the finest in the country by some degrees'. The story of the Wapping Ratcliff Highway Murders is retold in Peter Ackroyd's *Hawksmoor* (1985) and P. D. James and T. A. Critchley's *The Maul and the Pear Tree* (1990)

SPITALFIELDS

Spitalfields, to the east of Liverpool Street Station, was once the destination of French migrants fleeing from religious persecution. It is now a vibrant area with several popular markets, including Spitalfields, Brick Lane and Petticoat Lane.

Brick Lane

Brick Lane, once the destination of Jewish immigrants, is now home to Europe's biggest Bangladeshi community. Monica Ali's *Brick Lane* (2003) is set among the curry houses and Tower Hamlets high rise flats and tells the story of eighteen-year-old Nazmeen as she arrives from Bangladesh for an arranged marriage to a much older man. The novel explores how she adapts to her new community and begins to take control of her new life.

Brick Lane is a vibrant street usually crowded with people coming for curry, vintage shops and the market. Paolo Paradiso/shuttershock.com

WHITECHAPEL

Charles Dickens

Whitechapel was once a desperate and destitute area. In Charles Dickens' *The Pickwick Papers* (1837) Sam Weller and Mr Pickwick drink in the, now demolished, Bull Inn, and Sam observes Whitechapel is not, 'a very nice neighbourhood'. In *Oliver Twist* (1838), Fagin was inspired by a pickpocket known as the Prince of Fences who operated here in the 1820s.

Crime and Murder

Whitechapel was the scene of two of London's most notorious crime waves. Jack the Ripper murdered his victims here in the late nineteenth century. Then in the 1960s, Whitechapel was the heartland of the Kray twins and their gangland violence. The Ripper murders have inspired many books, including Marie Belloc Lownde's fictional retelling, *The Lodger* (1913). The Krays have also been featured in many books. Jack Arnott's novel, *The Long Firm* (1999), tells the story of Harry Starks, a gay East End gangster in the 1960s, and blends fiction with real-life characters, including the Krays and Judy Garland. In Truecrime Arnott retells the events around Ronnie Kray's funeral and follows the underworld of gangsters and criminals into the 1990s.

Jack the Ripper has inspired many crime and thriller writers. guidopiano/shuttershock.com

5

SOUTH LONDON

SOUTHWARK AND BANKSIDE

For centuries, London Bridge was the only bridge over the Thames and the only gateway into the south side of London. Southwark, just south of London Bridge, was once the first village outside of London. Bankside, stretching between London Bridge and Waterloo, is one of the city's main cultural centres, with Tate Modern, Globe Theatre and The Southbank Centre including The National Theatre and Festival Hall.

Blake's Bankside

Blake moved from Soho to 13 Hercules Buildings, close to the Waterloo end of Bankside. In 1791 this was a move away from the filthy, crowded city to the countryside. Blake and his wife, Catherine, lived here for nine years, some of Blake's happiest and most productive. The house has long been demolished, but Blake's time here is commemorated with mosaics of his most famous engravings on Waterloo's railway arches that now stand where the fields and trees of Blake's time once were.

William Shakespeare

Shakespeare's original Globe Theatre, on Park Street, just off Southwark Bridge Road, opened in 1599. Bankside's new Globe, a quasi-Elizabethan replica of

the original, has a permanent exhibition of 'Shakespeare's World' and hosts

One of a series of mosaics depicting Blake's most famous engravings under Waterloo's railway arches.

The full-sized effigy to Shakespeare at Southwark Cathedral. goga/shutterstock.com

productions of his plays throughout the year.

Shakespeare is honoured at Southwark Cathedral, where he is believed to have attended services, in an effigy and stained-glass window depicting scenes from his plays. The cathedral also has memorials to Geoffrey Chaucer, John Bunyan and Samuel Johnson.

The Borough and Little Dorrit

Now most famous for its market and as home to the lovelorn, diet-obsessed spinster in Helen Fielding's *Bridget Jones's Diary* (1996), Borough has a literary history dating back to 1400, when the pilgrims set off from a pub on the High Street in Geoffrey Chaucer's *The Canterbury Tales.*

Charles Dickens first came to Borough to visit his father in Marshalsea Prison in 1824. He lived on Lance Street with a kindly couple who later inspired Mr and Mrs Garland in *The Old Curiosity Shop* (1841). In *Little Dorrit* (1857), Amy Dorrit, 'a child of the Marshalsea' is born and raised in the prison. Amy is baptised at The Church of St George the Martyr, on Long Lane, Borough High Street. The church, also now known as 'Little Dorrit Church', has a window portraying her there.

Borough market, the oldest fruit and vegetable market in London, features in *The Pickwick Papers* (1837), where Bob Allen naps on the market office steps. In the same novel, Mr Pickwick meets Sam

Weller for the first time at the White Hart Inn, then on Borough High Street.

Nancy's Steps

The steps leading down from the west side of London Bridge to Southwark Cathedral are known as 'Nancy's Steps'. Many people come here believing this is where Nancy was killed at the hands of her brutal and merciless lover, Bill Sikes. A plaque was even here marking the spot of her death. Although the bridge and steps featured in Nancy's final scene in the famous musical film, in Dickens' novel *Oliver Twist* (1838),

Nancy's Steps, where she speaks with Mr Bronlow and Rose. Nancy is not killed on the steps in the novel.

Nancy arranges to meet Mr Bronlow and Rose Maylie on London Bridge and guides them down the steps so they can't be seen or heard. Here she tells the pair about Oliver's evil half-brother, Monks, so he can be arrested, and Oliver will be safe. But the meeting is overheard by Noah Claypole who tells Fagin and Sikes. Despite Fagin's pleas to Sikes not to be 'too violent', Nancy's kindness results in her murder, but it is in the lodgings the couple share, not out here on the bridge, that she is beaten to death.

London Bridge is presented in a more magical way in Virginia Woolf's *Orlando* (1928), when the young Orlando visits the Frost Fair of 1608. Woolf beautifully captures the atmosphere of the markets, dancing and jollity Londoners once shared on the frozen Thames.

The Anchor, Bank Side

This was a popular literary pub in the late 1700s with patrons including Oliver Goldsmith and James Boswell.

The George, George Inn Yard, 77 Borough High Street

One of London's oldest pubs and its only remaining galleried pub, The George dates back from 1676 and has retained the atmosphere of an authentic seventeenth-century coaching inn. Nicknamed 'Shakespeare's local' it shows his plays in the courtyard during the summer. Tip Dorrit writes a begging letter to Arthur Clannan here in Dickens' *Little Dorrit* (1857).

CAMBERWELL AND PECKHAM

Camberwell is a diverse area of London, with some of the city's grandest Georgian houses next door to blocks of twentieth-century social housing. Neighbouring Peckham is a cosmopolitan area built around its large green common, Peckham Rye.

Murial Spark moved to 13 Baldwin Crescent, Camberwell, in 1955 where she lived here in a cramped attic for eleven years. She finished her first novel, *The Comforters* (1957), here and wrote seven more, including *The Ballad of Peckham Rye* (1960), set in the area.

As a child in the 1760s, William Blake took long walks across Peckham Rye and had the first of the angelic visions that inspired much of his poetry and art here when he saw, 'a tree filled with angels, bright angelic wings bespangling every bough like stars'.

The much-loved children's author, Enid Blyton, was born near Peckham Rye, on Lordship Lane.

Peckham Rye. Stockimo/shuttershock.com

DEPTFORD

Deptford is another vibrant multicultural area of South London, with a busy market and where traditional pie and mash shops share streets with Caribbean cafés.

Christopher Marlowe was murdered here on 30 May 1593 when a disagreement over the bill after a long drinking session in the Deptford Tavern led to a dagger fight. Marlowe's death inspired Charles Nicholl's *The Reckoning* (1992) and Anthony Burgess' *Dead Man in Deptford* (1993), both of which imagine the widely held theory that Marlowe was assassinated as a spy. Marlowe is buried in an unmarked grave at St Nicholas' Church, near Deptford Railway Station.

A view across Deptford Railway Station to St Nicholas Church, where Marlowe is buried.
JohnGK/shutttestock.com

CLAPHAM

Famous for its busy railway junction, Clapham is a desirable family residential area with stylish shops and a common, as well as busy pubs and restaurants.

Graham Greene moved to 14 Clapham Common North Side in 1935, with his wife and two children. In 1940, Greene's family evacuated to Sussex, leaving the writer behind. Their home sustained heavy bombing in a raid soon after, but thankfully, Greene was unharmed. His survival was not a miraculous one. Greene had stayed the night at the home of a lover. Maurice Bendrix, the narrator of Greene's novel *The End of the Affair* (1951), lives in a bedsit on the 'wrong' side of Clapham Common.

The Windmill Hotel, South Side Clapham

This popular family and dog-friendly pub is fictionalised as 'The Pontefract Arms' in Graham Greene's *The End of the Affair* (1951). The Windmill was a favourite of Greene's during his time in Clapham and he would often carry jugs of beer across to his home on North Side to share with guests.

Angela Carter lived for sixteen years at 107, The Chase, Clapham, before her death in 1992. During this time, Carter had some major renovations done to the house and wrote to her agent that the stress was causing here to chew Valium 'like they were sweets'. She wrote *Nights at the Circus* (1984) and *Wise Children* (1991) here and tutored her student, Kazuo Ishiguro, on the kitchen table.

Oscar Wilde passed through Clapham Junction Station on his train journey from Pentonville Prison to Reading Gaol during a two-year sentence for indecency. He spent half an hour at the station, handcuffed and surrounded by a mocking crowd.

Clapham Common is now a desirable residential area, popular with families. Charles Bowman/shutterstock.com

BRIXTON

Brixton was once a nineteenth-century middle-class suburb and is now a hip and edgy centre of Jamaican culture.

Rebecca West grew up in Brixton at the end of the nineteenth century and charmingly depicts Edwardian Brixton in *The Fountain Overflows* (1957). Angela Carter set her last novel, *Wise Children* (1991), in a reimagined Brixton, following the fortunes of Dora and Nora Chance, the twin chorus girls who live on the 'bastard side of the Thames'.

On of Brixton's most important voices of recent times is Linton Kwesi Johnson (LKJ), one of Britain's most influential poets and social critics and the king of dub poetry, a style emerging from the reggae culture of 1970s Kingston, Jamaica. Johnson moved from Jamaica to London in 1963 and joined the Black Panthers movement while still at school. His poetry pioneered the written use of Jamaican dialect. In 2002, his collection, *Mi Revalueshanary Fren*, made LKJ the first black poet, and only the second

Brixton is a colourful, multicultural community, heavily influenced by Jamaican culture.
ElanaChaykinaPhotography/shutterstock.com

living poet, to be published in Penguin's *Modern Classics*. His *Selected Poems* were published by Penguin in 2006, a collection that depicts life in Jamaican London, from protests against police brutality to celebrations of urban life.

Alex Wheatle is a writer and poet best known for his novel *Brixton Rock* (1999), telling the story of Brenton Brown, a sixteen-year old overcoming the challenges of growing up as a young black man in south London at the time of the Brixton race riots in the 1980s. Wheatle has written many books continuing the stories of Brenton Brown, his family and friends amidst Brixton's rampant crime and simmering racial tensions. He revisits Brixton twenty years after the riots in *The Dirty South* (2011) and continues to write books about South London.

Candice Carty-Williams' *Queenie* (2020) follows a young Brixton journalist struggling to straddle Jamaican and British cultures.

CRYSTAL PALACE AND NORWOOD

Crystal Palace takes its name from the iron and glass structure built in Hyde Park for the Great Exhibition of 1851. The 'Crystal Palace' was moved here in 1854, where it remained in Crystal Palace Park until it was destroyed by fire in 1936.

In Angela Carter's wondrous novel, *The Magic Toyshop* (1967), Finn takes Melanie to see the remains of the palace. The pair then walk around Crystal Palace Park, past a fallen statue of Queen Victoria and across the white squares on a chessboard before Finn kisses Melanie and begins her conflicted feelings of attraction and understanding of the nature and boundaries of love.

Arthur Conan Doyle moved to South Norwood, downhill from Crystal Palace, in 1891, after the success of his early Sherlock Holmes novels enabled him to give up his work as an ophthalmologist and focus on writing. Here, he wrote many more, including *The Norwood Builder* (1903). In 1894, he married and moved to the country.

The Terrace at Crystal Palace Park.
Igor Matic/shutterstock.com

BECKENHAM AND BROMLEY

Enid Blyton moved to this well-to-do London suburb in 1925, following her marriage to Major Hugh Alexander Pollock in Bromley Registry Office.

Rat and Parrot (now Zizzi's), Beckenham High Street

Formally the Three Tuns, in Hanif Kureishi's *Buddha of Suburbia* (1990). Kamin Amir and his father arrive here and find a Kevin Ayres gig. Amir chooses the pub as it was where his hero, David Bowie, held his Beckenham Arts Lab. Kureishi mentions Bowie throughout the novel. The singer responded by writing the theme tune for the novel's television

David Bowie who lived in Bromley, performed on Beckenham Park bandstand in 1969.
Jono Photography/shutterstock

adaptation. Most of the *Buddha of Suburbia* is set in nearby Bromley.

H. G. Wells was born on Bromley High Street in 1866 and spent the first thirteen years of his life here. His former home at number 47 is currently a Primark Store. Wells refers to Bromley as 'Bun Hill' in *The War in the Air* (1908) and as 'Bromstead' in *The New Machiavelli* (1911). He mentions Beckenham in *Tono-Bungay* (1909). In 1934, Bromley offered Wells 'the freedom of the town', Wells, already had a distinction from The City of London and turned it down.

6

SOUTH WEST LONDON

BELGRAVIA, KNIGHTSBRIDGE AND PIMLICO

Belgravia, Knightsbridge and Pimlico, situated close to Victoria, are residential districts for the wealthiest in London. Sloane Square gave its name to the term 'sloane', describing stereotypical upper-class people, following an article in Harpers and Queen in 1975 about the affluent occupants of Pimlico, Kensington and Chelsea.

Sloane Street

Jane Austen stayed with her brother, Henry, and his wife, Eliza, at 64 Sloane Street. Henry helped Jane publish her work and the couple took her on theatre trips and to parties, giving her an insight into London society life. After Eliza died, Henry moved to a smaller flat at nearby 23 Hans Place, Sloane Street. Jane visited to look after Henry during a long period of illness between 1814 and 1815. When Jane died in 1817, her brother worked to shepherd her remaining novels, *Persuasion* (1818) and *Northanger Abbey* (1818), to print.

Sloane Street. goga18128/shutterstock

When the news was out, in 1895, that Oscar Wilde was about to be arrested for gross indecency, his friends advised him to flee the country. Out of a mixture of stubbornness and laziness, Wilde opted to stay at the Cadogan Hotel, Sloane Street. When the police arrived, they found him lounging about and smoking. The story was retold in John Betjeman's poem, *The Arrest of Oscar Wilde at the Cadogan Hotel* (1937).

Percy Bysshe and Mary Shelley stayed

at nearby 41 Hans Street in 1814 when they returned from their elopement in France. In February 1815, Mary gave birth prematurely to a baby girl who survived just a few weeks. Years later, Mary moved to number 24 in nearby Chester Square, where she died a widow from a suspected brain tumour in 1851.

Sloane Square Station

J. M. Barrie met the five Llewelyn Davies brothers while walking his dog in Kensington Gardens. Barrie befriended the family and the boys became the inspiration for 'The Lost Boys'. Barrie based Peter Pan on the eldest, Peter Llewelyn Davies. Davies hated the association and felt it troubled him throughout his life. In 1960, after sinking into depression, Davies spent a night drinking at the bar of the Royal Court Hotel and jumped in front of a train at Sloane Square Station. Papers broke the news with the headline, 'The Boy Who Never Grew Up is Dead'.

In Iris Murdoch's *A Word Child* (1975) Hilary Burde gets on the tube at Sloane Square to ride around the Circle Line. John Betjeman frequently used the same station and was known for travelling with his teddy bear, Archie, on his lap and talking to it. When people stared at him, the eccentric poet would tell the bear to behave as 'everyone's staring at you'. This story inspired Evelyn Waugh, who based Sebastian's relationships with his bear, Aloysius, on Betjeman and Archie in *Brideshead Revisited* (1945).

The Royal Court Theatre, Sloane Square, opened in 1956 with the premiere of John Osborne's *Look Back in Anger*. Harley Granville-Barker directed over 700 productions of George Bernard Shaw's plays between 1904 and 1907.

Sloane Square Station.
Sandor Szmutko/shutterstock.com

Known as the writer's theatre, The Royal Court still seeks and encourages new talent with workshops, commissions and a promise to read and consider every script it receives. Racquel Rodr/shuttterstock.com

Other notable premieres include Arnold Wesker's *Chips with Everything* (1962), Carol Churchill's *Serious Money* (1987) and Jez Butterworth's *Mojo* (1995).

Noël Coward lived in Belgravia's Gerald Road, at number 17, for sixteen years from 1930. In 1941, he returned home from a night out and was shocked to find his building and surrounding streets badly damaged from a bomb. Coward joined those out searching for casualties, inspiring his song, *London Pride*. With his home so badly damaged, Coward stayed at the Savoy Hotel for the remainder of the war, returning to Gerald Road once it was repaired. Coward wrote *This Happy Breed* here in 1943, as well as his autobiographical works, *Cavalcade* (1931), *Present Indicative* (1937) and

Future Indefinite (1954). He left the house in 1956 for Bermuda, saying it was sad for him to think he would never live in England again.

One of the most memorable scenes in Neil Gaiman's *Neverwhere* (1996) is the Floating Market at Harrods. The shop's management refused to allow the scene to be filmed there in Gaiman's television adaptation, so the market was filmed at Battersea Power Station.

KENSINGTON AND EARL'S COURT

Kensington is a stylish residential area of London and a popular place for writers to live, especially those juggling their work with London day-jobs and families. Nearby Earls Court is less luxurious, with more affordable housing and budget hotels.

Beatrix Potter

The treasured children's author, Beatrix Potter, was born and grew up in 2 Bolton Gardens, Kensington. The house was bombed out during the Blitz and, appropriately, rebuilt as a primary school, now Bousfield Primary. Another much loved children's writer and illustrator, Quentin Blake, lives nearby the school and calls in 'two or three times in the year for some reason for another', including the annual leavers' assembly.

Nancy Mitford

'Bright Young Thing' Nancy Mitford lived in her family home, 4 Rutland Gate Mews, during the Second World War when her husband was called to

duty. Part of the house was used during this time as a refuge for people made homeless in the bombings.

Virginia Woolf

Virginia Woolf grew up at 22 Hyde Park Gate with her siblings. Her mother, the Pre-Raphaelite model and philanthropist, Julia Stephen, died in 1895, when Woolf (then Stephen) was thirteen years old, leading to her first nervous breakdown. Julia's husband, the historian, biographer and mountaineer, Lesley Stephen, encouraged his young daughter to become a professional writer, before his death in 1904, which prompted the Stephen siblings to move to Bloomsbury.

T. S. Eliot

In the early 1920s, T. S. Eliot moved to a small flat at 9 Grenville Place, after returning to London from Buckinghamshire to work as a bank clerk at Lloyds. Virginia Woolf published his famous poem, *The Waste Land* under her and Leonard Woolf's Hogarth Press in 1922.

In 1957, Eliot moved back to Kensington with his new wife and former secretary Valerie, thirty-eight years his junior. The couple had a full and happy life at 3 Kensington Court before Eliot died in 1965. Valerie stayed until her death in 2012. The plaque commemorating Eliot's time here was unveiled by Ted Hughes in 1992.

William Makepeace Thackeray

William Makepeace Thackeray lived at 16 Young Street in 1846. Thackeray's daughters had lived with their grandmother in Paris since their mother's confinement to a private asylum in 1842. Once Thackeray settled here, they returned and the family resumed a relatively normal life, a happy reunion that inspired him to finish *Vanity Fair* (1847).

Earls Court in Fiction

In Andrea Levy's *A Small Island* (2004), Queenie lives at 21 Nevern Street, Earls Court, wondering if her husband will ever return from the war, and taking in Jamaican lodgers to help make ends meet, much to the disapproval of her neighbours.

Patrick Hamilton's *Hangover Square* (1941) was originally subtitled *A Tale of Darkest Earl's Court*. The story of George Harvey Bone and his infatuation with Netta is told against a backdrop of an hotel in Earls Court's 'grimy publands'.

CHELSEA AND FULHAM

In the nineteenth and early twentieth century, Chelsea was a stylish but bohemian area. By the end of the twentieth century, its bohemian residents had moved to Islington, Hampstead and Notting Hill, and Chelsea became a luxurious residential area. Many of London's wealthiest writers have lived here.

Agatha Christie

Agatha Christie lived at 48 Swan Court with her second husband for nearly three decades, from 1948 until her death in 1976. She wrote some of her most famous novels here, including *Third Girl*

Agatha Christie. spatuletail/shutterstock.com

(1966), a Poirot story set in Swan Court, with three girls living in a London flat, until one of them goes missing.

Cheyne Walk

Mary Anne Evans, who wrote under the name George Eliot, moved to 4 Cheyne Walk, just three weeks before her sudden death from flu just before Christmas 1880.

T. S. Eliot lived at Cheyne Walk, at 19 Carlyle Mansions, from 1946 to 1957 while he worked as an editor at Faber and Faber. He won his Nobel Prize for literature in 1948. Ian Fleming lived in a flat two floors above Eliot, with his wife and child, at number 24. His first Bond novel, *Casino Royale* (1953), was published while he was here. Another resident of Carlyle Mansions was

Henry James, where he finished two autobiographies and became a British citizen in 1915, a few months before he died.

Poet and artist Dante Gabriel Rossetti lived at 16 Cheyne Walk from 1862, following the death of his wife, the poet Elizabeth Siddal. Algemon Swinbourne stayed with him for a year, during which Rossetti had to tell him to stop making noise, sliding down the banisters with his boyfriend, and disturbing his painting. Rossetti also had a large collection of exotic animals and birds in his flat, including wallabies, a kangaroo, a racoon, a peacock, burrowing armadillos and a wombat. The peacock was evicted when neighbours complained about the noise. Charles Dodgson, a friend of Rossetti, better known as Lewis Carroll, was captivated by the wombat and included it as the dormouse in *Alice's Adventures in Wonderland* (1865).

Penelope Fitzgerald's *Offshore* (1979) is a wonderful novel about a community of house boaters at Battersea Reach, opposite Cheyne Walk.

A. A. Milne

A. A. Milne moved to 13 Mallord Street with his wife in 1919. His son, Christopher Robin, was born the following year. The first poem about Winnie-the-Pooh was published when the real Christopher Robin was four in *When We Were Very Young* (1924). This was followed by the bear's first full books of adventures,

Winnie-the-Pooh (1926), *Now We Are Six* (1927), written in Christopher Robin's sixth year, and *The House at Pooh Corner* (1928). Milne owned the house until 1942.

Bram Stoker lived at 18 St Leonards Terrace from 1885, where he wrote *Dracula* (1897) and *The Lair of the White Worm*, published in 1911, a year before his death.

P. L. Travers moved into 50 Smith Street, where she wrote *Mary Poppins in the Park* (1952), the fourth book in the series about the famous nanny. She was also negotiating with Disney during this time for her books to be transformed in the much-loved musical. Travers adopted a baby boy in 1940, from a family she knew in Ireland. In 1957, to her astonishment, her son's twin brother arrived at Smith Street. It was a shock to the son too, as not only was he unaware he was a twin, he didn't even know he was adopted.

Oscar Wilde's home on 34 Tite Street is the only one of the playwright's London homes to bear a blue plaque. He lived here with his wife and two sons and wrote *The Picture of Dorian Gray* (1890), his only novel here, drawing heavily on his experiences of hedonistic Victorian London.

Born in south London's Herne Hill, art historian Anita Brookner lived at 68 Elmtree Gardens during her fifties, when she began a new career as a novelist, writing a book a year from the age of fifty-three. Her first novel, *A Start in Life*, was published in 1981. Her fourth, *Hotel*

The statue of a famous Nanny, Mary Poppins, in Leicester Square. CK Travels/shutterstock.com

de Lac (1984), was awarded the Booker Prize. Brookner never married. When she died 2016, she left the house and her estate to the international medical charity, Medecins Sans Frontieres.

7

WEST LONDON

BAYSWATER

Bayswater encompasses Hyde Park and Paddington's stylish and exclusive residential terraces.

Peter Pan and the Darlings

The Llewelyn Davies family, who inspired Peter Pan and the Lost Boys, lived at 31 Kensington Park Gardens, the address J. M. Barrie gave the Darlings and where Peter first met Wendy and her brothers. J. M. Barrie lived nearby at 100 Bayswater Road between 1902 and 1909, and wrote most of *Peter Pan* in the summerhouse in 1904.

Hyde Park

The Serpentine features in Althea Hayter's *A Sultry Month* (1965), where she explains how an evening stroll along the lake could lead to a lethal fever at a time when raw sewage was pumped into its water. In Arthur Conan Doyle's Holmes story *The Noble Bachelor*, Hatty Doran's wedding clothes are found floating on the Serpentine before the lake is dragged for her body.

A real life drama that would have intrigued the famous detective occurred

A sculpture of the famous boy who never grew up can be found in Hyde Park, south of Marlborough Gate and Lancaster Gate. Anton_Ivanov/shutterstock.com

The Serpentine is a man-made lake in Hyde Park.
IR Stone/shutterstock

in the 1820s when a man was found hanging from a tree in Hyde Park, wearing a shirt marked 'S. T. Coleridge' Samiel Taylor Coleridge was later shocked to overhear two men in a coffee house talking about his terrible death. It turned out that the poor man had died wearing a shirt the poet had lost several years before.

Graham Greene features Hyde Park in *It's a Battlefield* (1934), where Drover is sentenced to death for stabbing a policeman he believed was about to attack his wife at a Communist rally.

Upper Class Bayswater

Many affluent writers have lived in the townhouses and terraces of Bayswater. Wyndham Lewis lived on Ossington Street in the 1930s, during which he had many affairs and contracted a variety of venereal diseases as a result.

Wilkie Collins moved to 30 Porchester Terrace with his family in 1830, where his father William, a painter, encouraged him to seek a job outside of the arts and sent him to be the apprentice of a tea merchant.

Nina Hamnet moved to 164 Westbourne Terrace after spending time in Paris. The artist joined The Bloomsbury Group and spent time drinking with Dylan Thomas at the Fitzroy Tavern. Hamnet published her memoir *Laughing Torso* in 1932. After her second book, *Is She a Lady?*, published in 1962, did not meet the acclaim of her first, Hamnet went on a drinking spree and fell or jumped out of her window, impaling herself on the fence below.

Paddington Station

Paddington Station is most famous for the place where The Browns find Paddington Bear in Michael Bond's *A Bear Called Paddington* (1958). There is a plaque and a statue of the famous bear on platform one, complete with his 'please look after this bear' label and suitcase containing marmalade sandwiches

In Agatha Christie's *4.50 From Paddington* (1957) and Graeme Greene's

It's a Battlefield (1934) and *The Ministry of Fear* (1943), Paddington Station is used as a scene of murder.

Hanan al-Shaykh portrays a different view of the area in *Only in London* (2002), following the lives of four people from four corners of the Arab world as their lives intertwine among the shawarma houses of Edgware Road.

The Paddington Bear statue at Platform One, Paddington Station. Aija Lehtonen/shutterstock

A Caribbean Festival was held in Notting Hill in 1958, following a spate of racial attacks, and has grown into today's Carnival.
Chris Mole/shutterstock.com

NOTTING HILL

Now a stylish and fashionable place to live, in the early twentieth century Notting Hill was once one of the most run down areas of London.

Multicultural Notting Hill

In the mid twentieth-century, Notting Hill became popular with the Windrush generation of Caribbean immigrants,

drawn by its cheap rents. Samuel Selvon's *The Lonely Londoners* (1956) centres around Notting Hill at this time and follows the lives of working-class Caribbeans trying to settle in their new lives.

Colin MacInnes' *Absolute Beginners* (1959) is set around Notting Hill in 1958 and portrays the changing world through the eyes of its new youth culture, learning about jazz music and race riots. Lynne Reid Banks' *The L Shaped Room* (1960) tells the story of an unmarried, pregnant woman who moves into a squalid bedsit with a Jewish writer, jazz musician and some prostitutes as neighbours. Alan Hollinghurst won the Man Booker Prize for *The Line of Beauty* (2004), about a gay student who finds lodgings in a 1980s Notting Hill mansion with a rising Tory MP, Gerald Fedden, and his family.

Thomas Hardy

Notting Hill was the home of a young Thomas Hardy who lived at 16 Westbourne Park Villas between 1836 and 1874. Here he wrote his first novel, *The Poor Man and a Lady*, completed in 1867 but never published after being rejected by five publishers.

HOLLAND PARK

Holland Park, on the western edge of central London, has been home to a diverse mix of London writers.

Agatha Christie

Agatha Christie moved to 47 Campden Street after her second marriage in 1930, where she wrote one of her most famous novels, *Murder on the Orient Express* (1934). She moved to nearby 58 Sheffield Terrace, where she lived until 1941 when the house was damaged in the Blitz.

Frances Hodgson Burnett

Frances Hodgson Burnett moved to 44 Lexham Gardens in 1884 where she wrote her much loved The Secret Garden (1911). Burnet moved to Portland Place after her eldest child, Lionel, died of tuberculosis in 1892

Siegfried Sassoon

The war poet, Siegfried Sassoon, lived at 23 Campden Hill Square between 1925 and 1931, where he wrote the first two novels in his semi-autobiographical trilogy, *Memoirs of a Fox-Hunting Man* (1928) and *Memoirs of an Infantry Officer* (1930).

Kenneth Grahame

Kenneth Grahame lived at 16 Phillimore Place, with his wife and son, while he was working at the Bank of England. He would tell his son bedtime stories about Ratty and Mole and their antics on the

The antics of Mole, Ratty and Badger grew from bedtime stories Kenneth Grahame told his son in Holland Park. Neftali/shutterstock.com

river that he eventually wrote in *The Wind in the Willows* (1908).

P. D. James

The crime novelist P. D. James lived at 58 Holland Park Avenue for thirty years from 1970, after her books earned her enough money to leave her job as a civil servant. She became Baroness James of Holland Park and sat in the House of Lords.

CHISWICK

Chiswick is a varied area of West London, from the picturesque Chiswick Village to the more suburbian Bedford Park, heading towards Ealing.

Anthony Burgess lived at 24 Glebe Street, Chiswick in the 1960s, where he wrote his biography of Shakespeare, *Nothing Like the Sun* (1964).

In Charles Dickens' *A Tale of Two Cities* the Lord Mayor of London is made to stand and deliver by a highwayman on Chiswick's Turnham Green.

Turnham Green, Chiswick.

Bedford Park

G. K. Chesterton set the opening of his novel *The Man Who Was Thursday* (1908) in Bedford Park. W. B. Yeats lived here twice, at 8 Woodstock Road for two years as a teenager and again at 3 Blenheim Palace Road, from 1888 to 1895, at a time when he was beginning to make his name in his early twenties.

HAMMERSMITH

Squeezed between the River Thames and the A4, Hammersmith has attracted some notable London writers.

William Morris

William Morris lived at Kelmscott House, 26 Upper Mall, from 1878 to his death in 1896, where he wrote and set his utopian novel set in the twenty-first century, *News from Nowhere* (1891).

Robert Graves

The poet and historical novelist Robert Graves lived at 35a St Peters Square in a bohemian menage-a-trois with his wife, Nancy, his lover, American poet Laura Riding, and Irish poet Geoffrey Phibbs. In 1929, Riding threw herself out of a third-storey window and broke her back. In a show of devotion, Graves ran downstairs, jumped out of an upper ground-floor window and twisted his ankle.

The Dove, 19 Upper Mall

The Dove is the oldest riverside pub in London and was among the favourite drinking places of Ernest Hemmingway and Graham Greene.

Peter Ackroyd

Peter Ackroyd grew up at 84 Wulfstan Street, at nearby East Acton, where he developed his love of literature and London. Ackroyd has since written countless biographies and novels about the city and its people, including many of the writers whose lives have been touched on in this book. *London: A Biography* (2000) and *Queer City* (2017) are among his most famous.

Kelmscott House, former home of William Morris, is now a museum dedicated to the textile designer, artist and writer.
Padmayogini/shutterstock.com

Novels, Poems and Writing Included

Aaronocitch, B. *Rivers of London*, 2011.
Ackroyd, P. *Hawksmoor*, 1985.
Ackroyd, P. *Dan Leno and the Limehouse Golem*, 1994.
Ackroyd, P. *The House of Doctor Dee*, 1993.
Ackroyd, P. *London: A Biography*, 2000.
Ackroyd, P. *The Clerkenwell Tales*, 2003.
Ackroyd, P. *Queer City*, 2017
Adams, D. *The Hitchhiker's Guide to the Galaxy*, 1981.
Ali, M. *Brick Lane*, 2003.
Al-Shaykh, H. *Only in London*, 2002.
Austen, J. *Sense and Sensibility*, 1811.
Austen, J. *Emma*, 1816.
Austen, J. *Persuasion*, 1818.
Austen, J. *Northanger Abbey*, 1818.
Arnott, J. *The Fatal Tree*, 2017.
Arnott, J. *The Long Firm*, 1999.

Bagnold, E. *National Velvet*, 1935.
Barnes, J. *Metroland*, 1980.
Barrie, J. M. *Peter Pan*, 1904.
Barrie, J. M. *Peter Pan*, 1911.
Bellec Lownde, M. *The Lodger*, 1913.
Bennett, A. *The Lady in the Van*, 1990.
Betjeman, J. *The Arrest of Oscar Wilde at the Cadogan Hotel*, 1937.
Blake, W. *Songs of Innocence and Experience*, 1789.
Bond, M. *A Bear Called Paddington*, 1958.
Bond, M. *Paddington at the Palace*, 1986.
Brookner, A. *A Start in Life*, 1981.
Brookner, A. *Hotel du Lac*, 1984.
Buchan, J. *The Thirty-Nine Steps*, 1915.
Butterworth, J. *Mojo*, 1995.
Burgess, A. *Dead Man in Deptford*, 1993.
Burgess, A. *A Clockwork Orange*, 1962.
Burgess, A. *Nothing Like the Sun*, 1964.

Burke, T. *Limehouse Nights*, 1916.

Carroll, L. *Alice in Wonderland*, 1865.
Carter, A. *The Magic Toyshop*, 1967.
Carter, A. *Nights at the Circus*, 1984.
Carter, A. *Wise Children*, 1991.
Cartland, B. *Virgin in Mayfair*, 1932.
Carty-Williams, C. *Queenie*, 2020.
Chaucer, G. *The Canterbury Tales*, 1400.
Chevalier, T. *Falling Angels*, 2009.
Chesterton, G. K. *The Man Who Was Thursday*, 1908.
Christie, A. *Murder on the Orient Express*, 1934.
Christie, A. *4.50 From Paddington*, 1957.
Christie, A. *Third Girl*, 1966.
Churchill, C. *Serious Money*, 1987.
Collins, W. *The Woman in White*, 1859.
Collins, W. *The Moonstone*, 1868.
Conan Doyle, A. *A Study in Scarlet*, 1887.
Conan Doyle, A. *The Sign of Four*, 1890.
Conan Doyle. A. *The Adventure of Wisteria Lodge*, 1917.
Conan Doyle, A. *The Illustrious Client*, 1925.
Conan Doyle, A. *The Man with the Twisted Lip*, 1891.
Conrad, J. The Secret Agent, 1907.
Coward, N. Cavalcade, 1931.
Coward, N. Present Indicative, 1937.
Coward, N. Future Indefinite, 1954.

Davies, W. H. *The Autobiography of a Super-Tramp*, 1908.
Defoe, D. *Robinson Crusoe*, 1719.
Defoe, D. *A Journal of the Plague Year*, 1722.
Defoe, D. *Moll Flanders*, 1722.
De Quincy, T. *Confessions of an English Opium Eater*, 1821.

De Quincy, T. *Murder Considered as One of the Fine Arts*, 1827.
Dickens, C. *The Pickwick Papers*, 1836.
Dickens, C. *Sketches by Boz*, 1837.
Dickens, C. *Oliver Twist*, 1838.
Dickens, C. *Nicholas Nickelby*, 1839.
Dickens, C. *Barnaby Rudge*, 1841.
Dickens, C. *The Old Curiosity Shop*, 1841.
Dickens, C. *American Notes*, 1842.
Dickens, C. *A Christmas Carol*, 1843.
Dickens, C. *Martin Chuzzlewit*, 1844.
Dickens, C. *Dombey and Son*, 1848.
Dickens, C. *David Copperfield*, 1850.
Dickens, C. *Bleak House*, 1853.
Dickens, C. *Hard Times*, 1854.
Dickens, C. *Little Dorrit*, 1857.
Dickens, C. *A Tale of Two Cities*, 1859.
Dickens, C. *Great Expectations*, 1860.
Dickens, C. *Our Mutual Friends*, 1965.
Dickens, C. & Thackeray, W. M. *The Loving Ballad of Lord Bateman*, 1839.
Dobbs, M. *The House of Cards*, 1989.
Dobbs, M. *Winston's War*, 2002.

Earlforward, H. *Riceyman Steps*, 1923.
Eliot, T. S. *The Waste Land*, 1922.
Evaristo, B. *Girl, Woman, Other*, 2019.
Falconer, H. *Primrose Hill*, 1999.

Fielding, H. *Bridget Jones' Diary*, 1996.
Fitzgerald, P. *Human Voices*, 1980.
Fleming, I. *Casino Royale*, 1953.
Fleming, I. *Diamonds are Forever*, 1956.
Forster, E. M. *Howards End*, 1910.

Gaiman, N. *Neverwhere*, 1996.
Galsworthy, J. *The Forsyte Saga*, 1922.
Grahame, K. *The Wind in the Willows*, 1908.
Greene, G. *It's a Battlefield*, 1934.
Greene, G. *Brighton Rock*, 1938.
Greene, G. *The Ministry of Fear*, 1943.
Greene, G. *The End of the Affair*, 1951.
Greene, G. *Went the Day Well, in The Last Word and Other Stories*, 1990.
Grissing, G. *New Grub Street*, 1891.

Grossman, G. & Grossman, W. *The Diary of a Nobody*, 1892.
Guo, X. *A Concise Chinese–English Dictionary for Lovers*, 2007.

Hall, R. *The Well of Loneliness*, 1949.
Hamilton, P. *Hangover Square*, 1941.
Buchan, J. *The Thirty-Nine Steps*, 1915.
Hayter, A. *A Sultry Month*, 1965.
Hensher, P. *Kitchen Venom*, 1996.
Hermes Gowar, I. *The Mermaid and Mrs Hancock*, 2016.
Hoban, R. *The Lion of Boaz-Jachin and Jachin-Boaz*, 1973.
Hodgson Burnet, F. *The Secret Garden*, 1911.
Hollinghurst, A. *The Line of Beauty*, 2004.
Hornby, N. *Fever Pitch*, 1992.
Hornby, N. *About a Boy*, 1998.
Huges, T. *18 Rugby Street, in Birthday Letters*, 1998.
Huxley, A. *Time Must Have a Stop*, 1944.

James, P. D. & Critchley, T. A. *The Maul and the Pear Tree*, 1990.
Johnson, L. K. *Mi Revalueshanary Fren*, 2002.
Johnson, L. K. *Selected Poems*, 2006,

Keats, J. *Ode to a Nightingale*, 1918.
Kemp, J. *London Tryptich*, 2010.
Kipling, R. *The Light that Failed*, 1891.
Kureishi, H. *The Buddha of Suburbia*, 1990.

Lamb, C. & Lamb, M. *Tales from Shakespeare*, 1807.
Lawrence, D. H. *The Rainbow*, 1915.
Lawrence, D. H. *Lady Chatterley's Lover*, 1928.
Le Carre, J. *Smiley's People*, 1979.
Lessing, D. *A Golden Notebook*, 1962.
Lessing, D. *London Observed*, 1992.
Levy, A. *Small Island*, 2004.
Lewis, C. S. *The Lion, The Witch and The Wardrobe*, 1850.
Lewis, W. *Apes of God*, 1930.

MacInnes, C. *City of Spaces*, 1957.

MacInnes, C. *Absolute Beginners*, 1959.
MacInnes, C. *Mr Love and Justice*, 1960.
McBride, E. *The Lesser Bohemians*, 2016.
McGrath, M. *Silvertown*, 2012.
McGrath, M. *Pie and Mash Down the Roman Road*, 2018.
Milne, A. A. *When We Were Very Young*, 1924.
Milne, A. A. *Winnie-the-Pooh*, 1924.
Milne, A. A. *Now We Are Six*, 1927.
Milne, A. A. *The House at Pooh Corner*, 1928.
Milton, J. *Paradise Lost*, 1667.
Milton, J. *Paradise Regained*, 1671.
Mo, T. *Sour Sweet*, 1982.
Morrison, A. *A Child of Jago*, 1896.
Morris, W. *News from Nowhere*, 1891.
Mortimer, J. *Rumpole of the Bailey*, 1978–2009.
Murdoch, I. *A Word Child*, 1975.

Nichols, C. *The Reckoning*, 1992
Niffenegger, A. *Her Fearful Symmetry*, 2010.

O'Neil, G. *Life in Cockney London*, 1999.
Orton, J. *Entertaining Mr Sloane*, 1964.
Orton, J. *Loot*, 1966.
Orton, J. *The Orton Diaries*, 1986.
Orwell, G. *Down and Out in Paris and London*, 1931.
Orwell, G. *Keep the Aspidistra Flying*, 1936.
Orwell, G, *The Road to Wigan Pier*, 1937.
Orwell, G. *Animal Farm*, 1945.
Orwell, G. *1984*, 1949.

Palliser, P. *The Prime Minister*, 1876.
Pepys, S. *Diary of Samuel Pepys*, 1665.
Pinter, H. *Betrayal*, 1978.
Pinter, H. *The Dwarfs*, 1963.
Plath, S. *The Bell Jar*, 1960.
Plath, S. *Ariel*, 1965.
Popoola, O. *When We Speak of Nothing*, 2017.
Priestly, J. B. *Angel Pavement*, 1930.
Priestly, J. B. *Let the People Sing*, 1930.

Reid Banks, L. *The L Shaped Room*, 1960.

Rowling, J. K. *Harry Potter and the Philospher's Stone*, 1997.

Sadler, M. *Fanny by Gaslight*, 1947.
Sassoon, S. *Memoirs of a Fox-Hunting Man*, 1928.
Sassoon, S. *Memoirs of an Infantry Officer*, 1930.
Self, W. *The Book of Dave*, 2006.
Selvon, S. *The Lonely Londoners*, 1956.
Shakespeare, W. *Henry VI, Part One*, 1590.
Shaw, G. B. *Mrs Warren's Profession*, 1893.
Shaw, G. B. *Caesar and Cleopatra*, 1898.
Shaw, G. B. *Man and Superman*, 1905.
Shaw, G. B. *Major Barbara*, 1905.
Shaw, G. B. *The Doctor's Dilemma*, 1906.
Shaw, G. B. *The Lady of the Sonnets*, 1910.
Shaw, G. B. *Pygmalion*, 1913.
Shelley, M. *Frankenstein*, 1818.
Smith, D. *101 Dalmatians*, 1956.
Smith, Z. *White Teeth*, 2000.
Smith, Z, *On Beauty*, 2005.
Smith, Z. *NW*, 2012.
Smith, Z. *Imitations*, 2020.
Spark, M. *The Ballad of Peckham Rye*, 1960.
Stevenson, R. L. *The Strange Case of Dr Jekyll and Mr Hyde*, 1886.
Stoker, B. S. *Dracula,* 1897.
Stoker, B. S. *The Lair of the White Worm*, 1911.
Storey, D. *Flight into Camden*, 1961.
Strachy, L. *Eminent Victorians*, 1918.
Symons, J. *The Blackheath Poisoning*, 1853.

Taylor, S. C. *Work Without Hope*, 1825.
Thackeray, W. M. *Vanity Fair*, 1847.
Townsend, S. *The Queen and I*, 1992.
Travers, P. L. *Mary Poppins*, 1934.
Travers, P. L. *Mary Poppins in the Park*, 1952.
Trollope, A. *Ralph the Heir*, 1871.

Walpole, H. *The Castle of Otranto*, 1764.
Waters, S. *Tipping the Velvet*, 1998.
Waugh, E. *Decline and Fall*, 1928.
Waugh, E. *Vile Bodies*, 1930.

Waugh, E. *Scoop*, 1936.

Waugh, E. *Brideshead Revisited*, 1945.

Wells, H. G. *The Invisible Man*, 1897.

Wells, H. G. *War of the Worlds*, 1898.

Wells, H. G. *The War in the Air*, 1908.

Wells, H. G. *Tono-Bungay*, 1909.

Wells, H. G. *The New Machiavelli*, 1911.

Welsh, I. *Stoke Newington Blues*, 1995.

Welsh, I. *Trainspotting*, 1993.

Wesker, A. *Chips With Everything*, 1962.

West, R. *The Fountain Overflows*, 1957.

Wheatle, A. *Brixton Rock*, 1999.

Wheatle, A. *The Dirty South*, 2011.

White, A. *Frost in May*, 1933.

Wilde, O. *The Picture of Dorian Grey*, 1890.

Wodehouse, P. G. *The Code of the Woosters*, 1938.

Woolf, V. *The Voyage Out*, 1915.

Woolf, V. *Mrs Dalloway*, 1925.

Woolf, V. *To the Lighthouse*, 1927

Woolf, V. *A Room of One's Own*, 1929.

Woolf, V. *The Waves*, 1931.

Wordsworth, W. *Upon Westminster Bridge*, 1802.

Worth, J. *Call the Midwife*, 2002.

Wyndham, J. *The Day of the Triffids*, 1951.

Wyndham, J. *The Midwich Cuckoos*, 1957.

Bibliography

Ackroyd, P. *T S Eliot*, Hamish Hamilton, 1984.

Ackroyd, P. *Blake*, Sinclair-Stevenson, 1995.

Ackroyd, P. *Dickens: Abridged*, Vintage, 2002.

Ackroyd, P. *Chaucer*, Chatto & Windus, 2004.

Ackroyd, P. *Wilkie Collins*, Chatto & Windus, 2012.

Alberti, F. B. *Writing Women's History and Westminster Abbey: The Case of Poet's Corner*, Historian's Watch, historyworkshop.com, 14 October 2019.

Baker, K. *London Lines: The Places and Faces of London in Poetry and Song*, Methuen, 1982.

Bedford, S. Aldous Huxley: A Biography, Papermac, 1993.

Birkin, A. *J. M. Barrie and the Lost Boys: The Real Story Behind Peter Pan*, Yale University Press, 2003.

Blackner, T. 'Lovers, Brothels and Modern Hypocrisy', *The Independent*, 29 September, 2004

Booth, M. *The Doctor, The Detective and Arthur Conan Doyle*, Hodder & Stoughton, 1997.

Briggs, J. *Virginia Woolf: An Inner Life*, Penguin, 2006.

Burgess, A. *You've Had Your Time*, Penguin, 1991.

Burgum, B. 'Bernardine Evaristo on BLM Activism, Feeling Invisible and Winning the Booker Prize', *Elle*, 4 September 2020.

Calloway, S. & Colvin, D. *The Exquisite Life of Oscar Wilde*, Orion Media, 1997.

Carpenter, H. *The Brideshead Generation, Evelyn Waugh and His Friends*, Weidenfeld & Nicolson, 1989.

Chaney, L. *Hide-and-Seek With Angels: The Life of J. M. Barrie*, Arrow, 2006.

Christie, A. *An Autobiography*, Harper Collins, 2017.

Churton, T. *Jerusalem: The Real Life of William Blake*, Watkins, 2020.

Coffield, D. *Tales from the Colony Room: Soho's Lost Bohemia*, Unbound, 2020.

Crick, B. *George Orwell: A Life*, Sutherland House, 2019.

Cruickshank, D. *Soho: A Street Guide to Soho's History, Architecture and People*, Weidenfeld & Nicolson, 2020.

Cunningham, I. *A Reader's Guide to Writer's London*, Prion, 2001.

Dakin, D. M. *A Sherlock Holmes Commentary*, David & Charles, 1972.

Davies, A. *Literary London*, MacMillan, 1988.

Denton, P. *Betjeman's London*, John Murray, 1998.

Dickens Hawksley, L. *Charles Dickens: The*

Man, The Novels, The Victorian Age, Welbeck Publishing, 2019.

Dickens Hawksley, L. Lizzie Siddal: The Tragedy of a Pre-Raphaelite Supermodel, Welbeck Publishing, 2017.

Dudgeon, P. & Ackroyd, P. Dicken's London: An Imaginative Vision, Headline, 1987.

Dyson, J. Dead Famous London, The Bluecoat Press, 2013.

Ellmann, R. Oscar Wilde, Penguin, 1988.

English Heritage. The English Heritage Guide to London's Blue Plaques, September Publishing, 2019.

Fisher, L. H. A Literary Gazetteer of England, McGraw, 1972.

Ford, M. Thomas Hardy: Half a Londoner, Mark Ford, 2016.

Foster, R. F. W. B. Yeats, A Life I, Oxford University Press, 1998.

Foster, R. F. W. B. Yeats, A Life II, Oxford University Press, 2005.

Flanders, F. The Victorian City: Everyday Life in Dickens' London, Atlantic Books, 2013.

Glinert, E. Literary London, Penguin, 2007.

Gordon, L. Five Women Writers Who Changed the World, Virago, 2012.

Gordon, L. The Imperfect Life of T. S. Eliot, Virago, 2012.

Greene, R. Russian Roulette: The Life and Times of Graham Greene, Little Brown, 2020.

Grice, E. 'Michael Dobbs, House of Cards Creator: Almost all Politicians Get Pushed', Financial Review, 19 March 2016.

Gristwood, S. Vita & Virginia: The Lives and Love of Virginia Woolf and Vita, Pavillion Books, 2018.

Hadley, T. 'Imitations by Zadie Smith Review: A Wonderful Essayist on the Lockdown'. The Guardian, 1 August, 2020.

Halliday, F. E. A Shakespeare Companion, Penguin, 1964.

Hamilton, J. The British Museum, The Landmark Library, Head of Zeus, 2018.

Hayter, A. A. Sultry Month, Scenes of London

Literary Life in 1846, Faber and Faber, 2011.

Hillier, B. John Betjeman: The Biography, John Murray, 2007.

Holland, M. & O'Conner, J. The Trials of Oscar Wilde, Samuel French, 2012.

Holmes, R. Shelley: The Pursuit, Harper Perennial, 2005.

Holroyd, M. Lytton Strachey: The New Biography, Pimlico, 2011.

Jackson, L. Walking Dickens' London. Shire Publications, 2012.

Jacobs, E. Kingsley Amis: A Biography, Hodder & Stoughton, 1995.

Janes, H. The Three Lives of Dylan Thomas, Robson Press, 2014.

Kolsky, R. Women's London: A Tour to Great Lives, IMM Lifestyle, 2018.

King, F. D. H. Lawrence and His World, Thames & Hudson, 1978.

Kitchen, P. Poet's London, Longman, 1980.
Lahr, J. Prick Up Your Ears: The Biography of Joe Orton, Bloomsbury, 2002.

Lee, H. Virginia Woolf, Vintage, 1997.

Lefebure, M. Thomas Hardy's World, Carlton, 1997.

Lewis, I. 'Author Bernadine Evaristo Says Some British People 'Still Don't Think Slavery Was Really a Bad Thing', The Independent, 17 June 2020.

Lessing, D. Under My Skin: Volume One of My Autobiography, to 1949, Fourth Estate, 1995.

Lessing, D. Walking in the Shade: Volume Two of My Autobiography, 1949–1962, Fourth Estate, 1998.

Lycett, A. Ian Fleming, Weidenfeld & Nicolson, London, 1995.

Lynskey, D. The Ministry of Truth: A Biography of George Orwell's 1984, Picador, 2019.
Manley, L. (Ed). The Cambridge Companion to the Literature of London, Cambridge University Press, 2011.

Mackenzie, N. & Mackenzie, J. The Time Traveller: The Life of H. G. Wells, Weidenfeld & Nicolson, 1973.

Meyes, J. Joseph Conrad: A Biography, Cooper

Square Press, 2001.

Motion, A. *Philip Larkin, A Writer's Life*, Hamish Hamilton, 1993.

Nicholson, V. *Among the Bohemians: Experiments in Living 1900–1939*, Harper Perennial, 2005.

Norrie, I. (Ed). *Writers and Hampstead*, High Hill Press, 1987.

Norton-Taylor, R. 'MI5 Spied on Doris Lessing for 20 Years Declassified Documents Reveal', *The Guardian*, 21 August, 2015.

Orton, J. *The Orton Diaries*. Methuen, 2013.

Plath, S. *The Journals of Sylvia Plath*, Faber and Faber, 2014.

Prince, A. *Kenneth Grahame: An Innocent in the Wild Wood*, Allison & Busby, 1994.

Rollyson, C. *The Last Days of Sylvia Plath*, University Press of Mississippi. 2020.

Ronsenbaum, S. P. *The Bloomsbury Group Memoir Club*, Palgrave Macmillan, 2014.

Rosnor, V. *The Cambridge Companion to the Bloomsbury Group*, Cambridge University Press, 2014.

Sheldon, M. Graham Greene: The Man Within, Heinemann, 1994.

Sheldon, M. *Orwell: The Authorised Biography*, 1991.

Shephard, R. *Sherlock Holmes's London*, CICO Books, 2015.

Smith, A. *John Buchan and His World*, Thames & Hudson, 1976.

Smith, J. *Being Betjeman (n)*, Galileo, 2020.

Smith, S. *J. K. Rowling*, CB Creative, 2013.

Spark, M. *Curriculum Vitae*, Constable, 1992.

Sturgis, M. *Oscar: A Life*, Apollo, 2018

Sturtevant, K. *Our Sister's London: Nineteen Feminist Walks*, The Women's Press, 1991.

Thornton, M. *The Decadent World of Graham Greene, The High Priest of Darkness*, The Daily Mail, 19 March 2008.

Thomas, C. *My Life With Dylan Thomas: Double Drink Story*, Virago, 2008.

Thompson, L. *Agatha Christie: A Mysterious Life*, Headline, 2020.

Tomalin, C. *Charles Dickens: A Life*, Penguin, 2012.

Top, S. *Eileen: The Making of George Orwell*, Unbound, 2020.

Tso, A. *The Literary Psychogeography of London*, Literary Urban Studies, 2020.

Vale, A. *A Woman Lived Here: Alternative Blue Plaques Remembering London's Remarkable Women*, Robinson, 2019.

Vaisittart, P. *London: A Literary Companion*, John Murray, 1988.

Varlow, S. *A Reader's Guide to Writer's Britain*, Prion, 2000

Viney, C. *Sherlock Holmes in London: A Photographic Record of Conan Doyle's Stories*, Smithmark Pub, 1995.

Wade, C. *The Streets of Hampstead*, High Hill Press, 1984.

Wagner-Martin, L. *Sylvia Plath: A Biography*, Lume Books, 2015.

Warren, A. Charles Dickens and the Street Children of London, Houghton Miffin Harcourt, 2017.

Werner, A. & Williams, T. *Dickens's Victorian London 1839–1901*, Ebury Press, 2012.

Williams, O. *The Secret Life of the Savoy: and the D'Oly Carte Family*, Headline, 2020.

Wilson, F. *Guilty Thing: A Life of Thomas De Quincey*, Bloomsbury, 2016.

Woolf, V. *A Writer's Diary: Being Extracts from the Diary of Virginia Woolf*, Harvest Books, 2003.